CREATIONS OF THE RAINBOW SERPENT

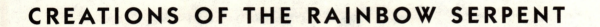

CREATIONS

OF THE RAINBOW SERPENT

Polychrome Ceramic Designs
from Ancient Panama

MARY W. HELMS

University
of New
Mexico
Press
Albuquerque

Library of Congress Cataloging-in-Publication Data
    Helms, Mary W.
Creations of the rainbow serpent: polychrome
ceramic designs from ancient Panama/
Mary W. Helms.—1st ed.
    p.   cm.
Includes bibliographical references and index.
ISBN 0–8263–1588–7 (cl)
1. Conte Site (Panama)
2. Indian pottery—Panama—Coclé (Province)
   —Themes, motives.
3. Indian pottery—Panama—Coclé (Province)
   —Classification.
4. Animals in art.
5. Indians of Central America—Panama
   —Coclé (Province)—Antiquities.
6. Coclé (Panama:Province)—Antiquities.
I. Title.
F1565.1.C6H45   1995
972.8'721—dc20
                95–3305
                CIP

*The following figures have been reproduced courtesy of
Dover Publications, Inc.: Figs. 3–6; 9–26a; 27–28a; 31;
33–34a; 35–36; 38–44; 46–47; 49–52; 54–70;
73–78; 82–84; 87–91a; 92a; 93a; 96–97; 99–100.*

CONTENTS

"... FOR RELIGIOUS MAN
NATURE
IS NEVER
ONLY
NATURAL."

MIRCEA ELIADE.
The Sacred and the Profane.
1959:151.

PREFACE

In the Preface and Introduction to his report on the Sitio Conte in central Panama, Samuel Lothrop describes the difficulties that had to be overcome in order to present the lavishly illustrated and textually detailed account of ceramic materials associated with this site (Lothrop 1942). These included sheer quantity of material, its poor state of preservation, its "innate complexity" and the "archaeologically abnormal conditions" under which it was found. Ceramic material was found in refuse, in caches, and as funeral furniture in graves. The quantities of sherds found as refuse had been greatly disturbed by the digging of grave shafts and/or perhaps by floods, and were of limited use. Cache and grave ceramics also posed problems, as Lothrop explains:

The amount of pottery deposited in individual graves varied greatly. ... We cannot give exact figures because the inhabitants of the Sitio Conte had (for the purposes of this study) several very unfortunate customs. One of these was the frequent "killing" of pottery vessels intended to accompany the souls of the dead, which was accomplished by trampling. The result of this was to reduce complete vessels to a compacted and intermingled mass of sherds. ... To make matters worse, these ceramic layers, which often were several inches in thickness when vessels had been piled one over the other, frequently were dug up and scattered when later burials were introduced. ...[1942:3–5]

The existence of compound graves and the practice of "robbing" older graves to provide additional goods for more recently deceased occupants added to Lothrop's problems (ibid.). These depositional circumstances resulted in several analytical difficulties, including "repairs which have been carried on more or less continuously for seven years, at times by several individuals" (ibid.: 5).

Lothrop speaks further about certain preparations of this material for publication, preparations that are pertinent to the following study, based as it is on Lothrop's illustrations:

A word must be said about illustrations. My feeling is that people are more interested in how things looked to the former Coclesanos than in how they look today. Restoration therefore has been carried out as far as possible in drawings, but the least uncertainty has either been indicated by dotted lines or has been noted in the text. For the same reason, photographs have been amply retouched. [ibid.: iii]

Lothrop then thanks, among others, Mr. William Baake who prepared the drawings and whose work, Lothrop properly notes, would be of permanent value in and of itself (ibid.). Additional scholars, including myself, who in succeeding decades have continued to be fascinated by the Sitio Conte ceramics, also owe a debt of thanks to Mr. Baake for the quality of his drawings, a selection of which is reproduced in this study.

In addition, I was fortunate to secure the services of Tim Barkley and especially Valerie Ward, Creative Services Division, Learning Resources Center, The University of North Carolina at Greensboro, whose photographic expertise reproduced most of the illustrations in this study. My sincere thanks to both of them. I also particularly wish to express my gratitude to Dr. Michael Robinson, director, National Zoological Park, Washington, D.C.; Ms. Margie Gibson, Office of Public Affairs, National Zoo; and Ms. Jessie Cohen, Graphics Department, National Zoo, for their generosity and kindness in helping with illustrations of the spectacled bear. The color illustrations of selected Coclé ceramics were compiled through the courtesy of the staffs of the Michael Carlos Museum at Emory University in Atlanta, Georgia, and of the Lowe Museum at the University of Miami at Coral Gables, Florida.

Readers who wish to know more about the details of the excavations of the Sitio Conte and especially the ceramics associated with the site are urged to consult Lothrop (1942). Although illustrations from that source are reproduced in this study, the original figures in Lothrop's publications (1942, 1976) should be consulted for nuances of color contrast or design that may have been unavoidably lost or reduced in reproduction here.

CREATIONS OF THE RAINBOW SERPENT

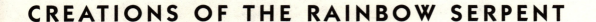

INTRODUCTION

In a well-known passage from Lewis Carroll's *Alice in Wonderland,* Alice muses upon the peculiarity of reading a book without pictures—seeking information and enjoyment from a series of tiny black spots arranged in lines upon a blank and generally colorless background. This predilection has bemused various non-literate peoples, too, when they first encountered book-reading Europeans. To some it seemed a particularly soulless activity, one that marked Westerners as peculiarly unidimensional and divorced from wider society, as living in another world (e.g., Hill and Wright, 1988:92–93). To literate Westerners, in turn, the modes of information management used by non-literate peoples can seem just as puzzling and just as difficult to decipher, even more so when the information system derives from prehistory and must stand alone, without the benefit of further explication by its makers.

This monograph attempts to fathom some of the semiotic characteristics of one such informational system that was encoded on a collection of polychrome ceramics thought to have been crafted approximately one thousand to fifteen hundred years ago (ca. A.D. 500-1100) by peoples of the so-called Coclé culture who lived in central Panama. Many of these wares were excavated at the Sitio Conte, a site on the banks of the Río Grande de Coclé in Coclé Province, central Panama (Fig. 1; see Linares 1977:34–38), by Samuel Lothrop in the 1930s (Hearne 1992:3). They were found in caches and burials directly associated with persons of high status, elites of some of the ranked and centralized societies or chiefdoms that were developing in Panama by at least A.D. 500 (Linares 1977:31; Cooke 1984:270–271, 287). They and similar ceramics from neighboring regions of the Azuero peninsula and

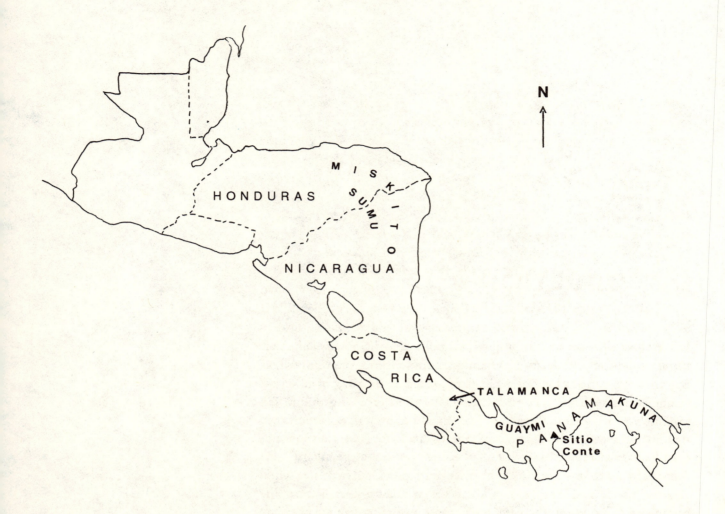

N

HONDURAS

M I S K I T O

S U M U

NICARAGUA

COSTA
RICA

TALAMANCA

GUAYMI

P A N A M A KUNA

Sitio
Conte

FIG. 1. *Indigenous peoples of Central America and the Sitio Conte, Panama.*

southwestern Panama are described and illustrated in Part II of Lothrop's *Coclé: An Archaeological Study of Central Panama* (1942) and also appear without text in a separate publication, *Pre-Columbian Designs from Panama* (Lothrop 1976). These two publications formed the basis for this study and reference will frequently be made throughout to one or other volume particularly to alert readers to additional designs that are not reproduced in this work. Since the 1976 work, *Pre-Columbian Designs from Panama,* is the more readily available, most references to additional designs will be made to that source.

The Coclé ceramic wares are characteristically multicolored and combine geometric forms with lively, very graphic depictions of curious birds and beasts. In typologies of prehistoric Panamanian ceramic styles they are designated as Conte polychrome (ca. A.D. 500–800) and as Macaracas polychrome (ca. A.D. 800–1100), but I will refer to them simply as Coclé polychromes since the finer stylistic distinction is not pertinent to this analysis (see Cooke 1985).

The ceramics are currently housed in Harvard University's Peabody Museum of Archaeology and Ethnology. Other pieces from the Sitio Conte are in the collection of the University Museum of the University of Pennsylvania (Hearne and Sharer 1992:13, 126). Numerous other examples of Panamanian polychrome wares exist in private holdings and in various museum collections (cf. Dade 1961; Lothrop 1942:iii), but only the Coclé ceramics excavated by Lothrop from Sitio Conte and related pieces also illustrated and discussed by Lothrop in his 1942 and 1976 publications are used in this study.

The pre-Columbian ceramic art of central Panama has been the subject of monographs by Lothrop (1942) and Olga Linares (1977). Lothrop's extensive analysis focused on classification and description based primarily on shape and secondarily on design (1942:11) and included attempts to identify components of zoomorphic patterns. Linares examined formal details of construction and design but has also suggested the possibility that identification of the zoological motifs of Coclé designs, based as they are on elements of nature, may be correlated with the social and political life of the Coclé culture.

More specifically, Linares considers it likely that "some of the motifs on Sitio Conte objects carried connotations of rank" and that the animals depicted were also symbolically related to status and rank (1977:61). She is particularly impressed by behavioral qualities of animals portrayed in this art, noting that they are poisonous or toxic or otherwise dangerous or predatory (1977:63–67), and suggests that "the central Panamanian art style was centered on a rich symbolic system using animal motifs metaphorically to express the qualities of aggression and hostility that characterized the social and political life" in central Panama at this time (1977:70).

In the analysis presented here, I concur to some extent with the symbolic and political-ideological components of Linares' perspective. However, rather than taking an overtly "etic" position (i.e., offering an interpretation based solely on the investigator's own perceptions and postulates of alleged behavioral parallels in depicted animal forms and human populace). I seek to interpret ceramic motifs from a more ethnographically based or "emic" perspective. Accepting the dictum that "all art is metaphor and form" (Vansina 1985:11), I wish to view Coclé designs as a semiotic code expressing sociological and especially cosmological concepts that also may have had some bearing upon the ideology legitimizing the status and activities of political elites.

Although it is obviously impossible to ascertain directly the political, ideological and cosmological concepts held by ancient Panamanians, it may be possible to suggest some general themes by seeking parallels in the exegesis of ethnographically known art forms and design motifs of still-extant indigenous cultures of the Americas. Research in the art styles of numerous native American cultures has shown that traditional artistic styles of all the Americas provide tangible means for expressing indigenous conceptualizations of the nature of the cosmos and the place of human society and especially society's leadership therein (e.g., Whitten and Whitten 1988; Rabineau 1975; Schele and Miller 1986; Goldman 1975; Berrin 1978; Penney 1985:180–98; Morphy 1989). These conceptualizations are frequently expressed in metaphors utilizing naturalistic phenomena of the heavens, the rivers, and the ocean, and the terrestrial and subterrestrial realms. I propose that the polychrome ceramic art of central Panama contains and conveys the same type of information. Consequently, in seeking to decode the cosmological-cum-political messages and metaphors this art expresses I will draw heavily upon indigenous American mythemes and symbolism from a range of cultures. By means of such comparisons it should be possible to identify at least the types of information the art of ancient Panama may be expected to express and to gain some idea of the general content of the messages contained in such graphic symbolic displays.

In pursuing this approach it is also necessary to consider not only the identification of the motifs depicted on the Coclé art and the possible symbolism contained therein but also the significance of the use of a chromatic style of painting per se, the possible significance of at least some of the ceramic shapes employed in this art, and the significance of the production of polychrome ceramics as a type of skilled craft replete with inherent aesthetic appeal for those who made, used, and viewed these pieces. Let us begin with the latter concern and briefly consider the general significance of skilled crafting and of aesthetics in traditional society by way of providing a general context for further appreciation of the polychrome ceramics of Panama themselves.

I apply the term "skilled crafting" to the production in traditional society of goods or art forms created by what are regarded as exceptional crafting skills. Such goods or art forms also usually serve non-utilitarian (that is, non-domestic, non-private) ceremonial, prestige-related, or public purposes. Skillfully crafted things are imbued *by definition* with qualities of honor and morality expressed as aesthetics, and they are closely associated with public political-ideological activities and symbolism. Such goods are crafted by talented artisans whose exceptional abilities are universally believed to derive from artistic creative skills first evidenced and/or taught to humans by ancestral culture-hero/creators at the time of origins of human societal existence when the power of the creators' songs or dances created the dry land, or their skills as smiths or sculptors or drummers brought humans into existence (Helms 1993a:chap. 2).

By expressing the same creative skills, contemporary living artisans, in the pursuit of their art, are believed to express a direct link to the original creator-beings. Like religious personnel, they are perceived as standing between society and the cosmological realm that lies beyond. Such skilled artisans serve as repositories for much esoteric knowledge concerning the means (both technical and ritual) by which acts of skilled crafting, as creative acts of transformation, shaping and forming, ordering and controlling, link society with the supernatural forces and energetics of the cosmological outside world that are believed to sustain society if they, too, can be ordered and controlled and put to beneficial human use. With this knowledge and by the use of their skills, such artisans also become living culture-hero/creators themselves, and their acts of crafting are believed actively to perpetuate and replicate "original" cultural creations. In so doing they not only represent but also maintain a direct living connection between the here-and-now of the current cultural setting and the there-and-then of outside space-time (Helms 1993a:chaps. 3 and 4).

In directly comparable fashion, political elites who sponsor or subsidize master artists in their work or, as is frequently the case, are master artisans themselves,[1] are similarly linked to the ancestral conditions of cultural-cum-cosmological beginnings. Skilled crafting directly and tangibly relates and connects artisans and their politically prominent sponsors to cosmologically defined times of cultural origins and occasions of social creation. Such associations do much to legitimize the political authority of elites by relating them to undeniable and unfalsifiable ideological First Principles (Helms 1993a:chap. 5).

The qualities and political-ideological values attributed to skilled crafting are also based on qualities associated with the meaning of aesthetics. Aesthetics in traditional society essentially refers to that which is both beautiful *and* morally good. Aesthetics expresses "truth" in terms of what is "right" and "proper" in thought (philosophy), action (ethics), and design (art). Here again, that which is considered "proper" and "right" derives from the principles of order deemed inherent in the nature of the gods or of the universe and from the expression of that order in rules or canons of form and design prescribed by tradition and/or authority (Coomaraswamy 1935:16–17; Helms 1993a:61-68).

Since morality and thus aesthetics are essential components of proper social living, tangible expressions of these principles would be expected to be highly valued. This is to say that the acts and products of skilled artisanry are valued in large part because they are aesthetic acts and products. Indeed, the very concept of *skilled* crafting as opposed to production of more mundane utilitarian goods lies in identification of the skilled artisan as one who can create or instill the aesthetically proper design, form, and feeling in his work.

The attraction of aesthetics—of that which is morally good—also rests on the fact that beauty is thought not only to be instructional and exemplary but also to have a supernatural sort of power, a dynamic, of its own (Helms 1993a:63). For that reason, too, persons of influence, being concerned with all aspects of power, are drawn to associate with aesthetics and, through beauty, with ultimate truths that both guide proper social living and confirm the legitimization of their political and ideological authority (Howard 1991).

Judging by the highly decorated nature of the Coclé polychrome ceramics, by the sophistication of the designs portrayed thereon, and especially by the fact of their association, by burial, with persons of apparently high status, it seems safe to consider these vessels as products of skilled crafting and as goods believed to embody the quality of aesthetics. They were presumably made by skilled artisans whose work was considered to be directly and inalienably related to cosmological times and conditions. If these suppositions be granted, then it also seems reasonable to seek guidelines to the identities and symbolic significance of the design motifs portrayed in this art within the field of traditional native American art, cosmology, and political-ideology.

COLOR PLATES

The forked tongue and long serpentine body form with sequential sets of parallel lines identify the serpent, specifically the boa constrictor, as an inherent quality of this legged saurian. The eye bars may also refer to the eye streaks characteristic of the boa. The long "chin whiskers" suggest a mytheme associating the serpent with Sibu, a Talamancan (Costa Rica) supernatural being. (Photograph by Edward M. Pio Roda, courtesy Michael C. Carlos Museum, Emory University, Coclé bowl, 1990.11.296.)

LEFT: *The banded tail identifies the zoological referent of the elaborately crested creature as the curassow. This painting also exemplifies the effective use of multiple colors to differentiate constituent design elements. (Photograph by Edward M. Pio Roda, courtesy Michael C. Carlos Museum, Emory University, Coclé plate, L1991.5.1.)*

ABOVE: *The curvilineal body lines of this elegant portrayal imply a serpent association, as does the double-headed or head-end-equals-tail-end design style, which uses V-elements most effectively. The "darts" emanating from the figure may be tangible renderings of the supernatural energy or potency with which both the creature and its painted portrayal are endowed. (Photograph by Edward M. Pio Roda, courtesy Michael C. Carlos Museum, Emory University, Coclé pedestal bowl, 1990.11.292.)*

ABOVE: *In this evocative use of kennings, large eyes, open jaws, eye stripe, and stylized claws were all that were needed to represent a distinctive creature to those who understood the pictorial "shorthand." (Photograph by Edward M. Pio Roda, courtesy Michael C. Carlos Museum, Emory University, Coclé pedestal bowl, L1994.1.4.)*

RIGHT TOP: *The sequence of rectangles and bar line sets in the center panel of this pedestal bowl abstractly references the body markings of the boa constrictor. The rounded shoulder and rump and length of tail suggest the animal in the hemispheres is a feline. (Photograph by Edward M. Pio Roda, courtesy Michael C. Carlos Museum, Emory University, Coclé pedestal bowl, 1990.11.294.)*

RIGHT BOTTOM: *The concentric circular patterning on the shell of this crustacean may depict a cross-section of the Tree of Life, from whose watery interior sea creatures first emerged after the Tree was felled. Alternatively, the circular patterning may reference the boa oval. (Photograph by Edward M. Pio Roda, courtesy Michael C. Carlos Museum, Emory University, Coclé bowl, 1990.11.289.)*

Double spout vessel **LEFT** with abstract design representing boa ovals, each containing a creature. The double spouts may reference the double-headed serpent motif. If the design band on the spouted vessel is compared with the red central band on the plate **RIGHT**, the double spouts appear to duplicate the two quarters of a plate hemisphere, each of which, by color coding, can also be seen to depict a creature-cum-serpent head. (Photograph courtesy Lowe Art Museum, Miami University, Coclé bowl, 93.0043.01, and Coclé double spout vessel, 93.0043.02.)

The female being painted on this effigy figure may depict the Great Mother as referenced zoologically by the spectacled bear. (Photograph courtesy Lowe Art Museum, Miami University, Coclé vessel, 89.0117.)

1   CHROMATICS

One of the most ubiquitous characteristics of the Coclé ceramics is that they are decorated in multiple colors, that they are polychromed. Let us begin analysis of this art by considering some of the symbolism accorded in native belief systems not just to different colors but to multiple colors expressed as a system, that is, to chromatics itself. As Hill notes (1992:117), all manner of brightly colored and iridescent natural phenomena can and have served as chromatic symbols in thought systems of traditional societies of the Americas (and elsewhere), including colored flowers, rainbows, hummingbirds, butterflies and other colorful and iridescent insects, shells, crystals, colored lights, flames, and dawn and sunset. Indeed, "the use of chromaticism in the construction of spirituality is so widespread that it must represent a very ancient level of religious thought" (ibid.:118). It seems reasonable to assume, therefore, that polychrome coloration itself carried symbolic significance in the ideological-cosmological world of the ancient Panamanians.

Insightful interpretations of the symbolism accorded to chromatics by indigenous societies of South America have been suggested by Gerardo Reichel-Dolmatoff and by Claude Lévi-Strauss (see also Hill 1992 regarding chromatics in the symbolism of the Southwest and Mesoamerica). South American ethnology may be particularly useful for an investigation of Panamanian ceramics since the native chiefdoms of Panama appear to have been linguistically related to, and politically associated with, northern South American cultures.[1]

Reichel-Dolmatoff's investigations among the Desana of the Vaupés territory of the Columbian Northwest Amazon have revealed an indigenous thought system in which different colors convey different manifestations of vital cosmic energy. White is contrasted with black as constituting different sets of "energies": white, in association with the heat and light and brilliance of the sun, appears as a generalized, life-giving force that pervades the entire universe; black, associated with the moon, bears energies associated with darkness and cold and, therefore, death. Other colors, or color energies, originate from these two extremes or are qualified by them. Their appearance or, better said, their designation by the Desana to different plants and animals (a designation that need not be in accord with the physical coloration of the subject) expresses the proportionate distribution of sun- and moon-derived energies in various circumstances and settings (Reichel-Dolmatoff 1978a:256–263 and passim).[2]

Claude Lévi-Strauss, in turn, regards chromatics either in color or in sound as means to express concepts of order versus disorder. He notes that chromatics in color generally has stood conceptually between white (symbolically as well as physically the summation of all color) and black (the absence of color and especially of light) as an elaboration of diversity. Chromatics presents a multihued enrichment of light sandwiched between the two single, monolithic, and achromatic signs of blackness and whiteness (Lévi-Strauss 1969:280). As such, polychromaticism can be interpreted from two perspectives: it can be seen as a differentiated series or gradation of "short-intervaled" steps moving along something of a continuum, as colors shade one into another, or it can be viewed as delineating multiple separate and distinct or "long-intervaled" units or contrastive sets, each a distinctive color sharply bounded and set off from the others, that then may be ordered into a coherent or structured system.

The first perspective, that of the continuum (represented by confusing shadings or jumbled color combinations), corresponds to the absence of structure and the lack of boundaries. If multiple colors are shaded gradually one into the other, the resulting continuum appears shapeless and formless, lacks order, and appears chaotic in nature. In contrast, the second perspective, that of discrete and distinct entities (seen in separate or block delineation of solid, bold, definitive colors) corresponds to clear differentiation of parts and, thus, to order. If multiple colors are depicted as solidly colored contrastive units, the clear boundaries separating each colored unit and the distinctiveness of each unit itself give shape and form, definitive order and organization, to the overall composition (Lévi-Strauss 1969:325; see also Classen 1990:725).

Lévi-Strauss illustrates his interpretation with reference to a common theme in native South American myths regarding the original creation of the distinctive colors and sounds (calls) of various birds and animals which allow them to be clearly differentiated from one another "zoologically" and thus to serve as statements of zoological/cosmological order. The myths derive these distinctive calls and markings from a prior condition of formlessness or shapelessness or fateful disjunction. Frequently the distinctive markings appear when the heretofore chromatically undistinguished creature is touched by the blood of a demolished Great Serpent, a creature lacking limbs or wings or fins or other means of differentiating (giving shape to) its inherently formless bodily continuum. For example, in an Arecuna tale, a young boy who had caught an excessive number of fish was himself killed by a huge water snake (a manifestation of the rainbow) that lived at the bottom of the pool. The snake was killed in turn and hauled onto dry land by the combined efforts of various birds, animals and men. The serpent's body was then skinned and cut into pieces, which the plunderers shared out among themselves.

According to the nature and color of the portion allotted to each one, the animals acquired the cries, the anatomical peculiarities, the coats, or the plumage that were henceforth to be characteristic of each species. [Lévi-Strauss 1969:262]

In such fashion, the white egret, the kingfisher, the toucan, the curassow, the macaw, the tapir, the deer, the agouti, the anteater, indeed all the wild animals, received their colored coats and plumage and distinctive "flutes" or calls (Lévi-Strauss 1969:302–303).

Similar tales abound among a number of other groups (Lévi-Strauss 1969:303–305; Lévi–Strauss 1973:229; Campbell 1989:81–82; Pressman 1991), although it is not always the rainbow snake who is responsible for creating this polychromed zoological order. Multicolored plumage can be derived from the blood of the moon or from the body of a demolished terrapin or from the battered remains of an angry old man who was carried off by eagles or from the blood of the wound caused when the sloth lost its tail (Lévi–Strauss 1969:312, 313–314, 317; Pressman 1991:84, 85). Finally, let us note a mytheme attributing distinctive colorations to the blood of a severed human limb. This myth is particularly interesting because the tale also includes decorated (polychromed?) ceramics. One version from the Caduveo goes as follows:

Three children used to play in front of the hut until past midnight. The father and mother paid no attention to them. One night when they were playing—it was very late—an earthenware pot descended from the sky; it was lavishly decorated and full of flowers.

The children saw the flowers and wanted to take them, but as soon as they put out their arms, the flowers retreated to the other side of the pot, with the result that the children had to climb into the pot in order to reach them.

The pot started to rise into the air. When she saw what was happening, the mother just managed to grab the leg of one of her children. The leg broke, and from the wound flowed a lake of blood in which most of the birds (whose plumage was at that time uniformly white) dipped either all or some of their feathers, thus acquiring the different-colored plumage they have today. [Lévi-Strauss 1969:302; see also Pressman 1991:85]

These myths are of considerable interest within the context of Coclé ceramics. Color as an ordering device and the colorful decoration of ceramics are obviously involved (Fig. 2). The severed-leg theme will also appear, and the theme of the serpent will be found to be as fundamental to many of the Coclé polychrome ceramics as the theme of color itself. In fact, given the importance of the serpent in this art, let us conclude this chapter by considering the mythological Great Snake of South American tales in more detail.

In zoological terms, the Great Snake of tropical South America is the anaconda (Roe 1989), mythologically credited in its primordial form not only with giving chromatic order to the realm of birds and beasts but also with the creation of humans from its great body as it swam upstream, creating human settlements and people wherever it stopped on its voyage (Hugh-Jones, 1977:192–193). The Great Snake of mythology is also conjoined with the Milky Way and the rainbow (Carlson 1982:151–159; Lévi-Strauss 1969:246–247, 297),[3] the latter sometimes said to be the serpent's feather crown (de Civrieux 1980:52), in a range of conditions including the onset of beneficial rain when the earth and the sky are conjoined by the fall of water from above, the destructive rain of hurricanes (this theme is particularly characteristic of Central American and Caribbean myths),[4] and the cessation of rain when the rainbow itself arches above the horizon in an orderly display of colors (cf. Tedlock 1984:256). The end of rain also annually announces the advent of the dry season, a maleficent condition seen as conducive to illness when sky and earth are *dis*joined by lack of rain, and the rain-

FIG. 2. *Color key for Sitio Conte ceramics. From Lothrop (1942: viii).*

bow is again frequently identified with serpentness, but now as multi-colored and deadly (Roe 1989; Lévi-Strauss 1969:115–116, 246–247; Lévi-Strauss 1973:80–81, 286–287, 380, 400; Reichel-Dolmatoff 1978a:266; Karsten 1968:359–361).[5]

The rainbow serpent is also implicated in the origins of polychrome ceramics. In this capacity the rainbow serpent stands as original "Owner of Designs" (Roe 1989) and as Master of potters' clay (Lévi-Strauss 1969:247; Lévi-Strauss 1988:183–184). The serpent also appears as the skilled creator who teaches the human ceramic artist how to combine color and clay so as to achieve aesthetic quality in her clay vessels. For example, in a brief tale from Amazonia on "The Origin of Painted Earthenware," a helpful snake teaches the necessary artistic skills to a young potter who originally was so inept at making pottery that her relatives laughed at her. One day a kindly old woman appeared and taught the unhappy potter how to make magnificent pots. On taking her leave the kind-hearted old woman told the potter that she would henceforth appear in the form of a snake but that the young woman should not be afraid and should embrace the snake. When, at its next appearance, the young woman did so, the snake at once turned into a "sprite" who showed her protégée how to paint earthenware pots with multicolored (yellow and brown) clays and with urucu (a red paint dye prepared from *Bixa orellana*). With these clays and paint "she drew beautiful variegated patterns" and told the young woman that "the kind of painting that draws the lizard's head, the Great Snake's tracks, the branch of the pepper tree, the breast of Boyusu the rainbow serpent, etc., is what we call Indian painting" and is different from the kind of painting that consists in painting flowers (Lévi-Strauss 1969:322–323).[6]

In this myth, as in many others, the serpent also contains phallic connotations related to the theme of illicit relationships (Lévi-Strauss 1988:25). The snake is further associated with fertility and life in its broadest sense, including the theme of immortality occasioned by the periodic shedding of its skin (Lévi-Strauss 1969:155). There are many tales discussing the endless rejuvenation achievable by lizards, serpents, or trees as contrasted to the loss of this ability by humans as a result of some unfortunate failing. Characteristic of this genre is a brief Amazonian tale whereby the snake, before rising into the sky to become the rainbow, urges people to preserve their immortality by listening for and replying to calls he will shout down from above, but regrettably, since they are asleep, they do not hear him (Lévi-Strauss 1969:161).

2   THE SERPENT

Drawing inferences both from archaeology and from the accounts of early-sixteenth-century Spanish conquistadors (Helms 1979), art, that is aesthetics, was ubiquitous in pre-Columbian Panamanian life, as it has been for native American societies in general. Language became an aesthetically pleasing art form in song, chant, and chiefly oratory. Body movements were transformed into dance. Daily behavior was shaped by the graces of etiquette. The human body was draped with finely woven and patterned textiles and adorned and painted in other ways. Chiefly dwellings in particular were carved and painted, and chiefly persons were adorned with golden and feathered ornaments, while polychrome or other forms of decorated ceramics replaced ordinary wares on ceremonial occasions, including chiefly funerals and interments.

Color coding appears to have played basic semiotic and epistomological roles in much of this art, especially that of the Coclé era ceramics. More specifically, Lévi-Strauss' "long-intervaled" expression of chromatics is readily evidenced in the Coclé polychromes since it is apparent that blocks of different colors—light and dark reds, purple, blue/black, and occasionally brown (Lothrop 1942:viii, 13, 194; see Fig. 2)—in the form of juxtaposed solid color units give form and order to the ceramic designs (Reichel-Dolmatoff's explication of color-coded energetics will be applied later in conjunction with the theme of luminosity). Some of these orderly and colorful depictions are geometric in design, but many depict curious creatures in which the blocks of solid color separate, differentiate, and contrast basic design units, that is, are used to identify and differentiate head crests, paws, claws, tails, beaks, central body forms and other units, one from the other.

FIG. 3. *Serpent. From Lothrop (1976:27).*

FIG. 4. *Bird with serpent body form and severed-leg motif. From Lothrop (1976:46).*

Often the order expressed in these depictions is accomplished by providing limbs and feet, tail and head crest, to a basic body form that is serpentine in nature. This basic serpentine form is distinguishable because it is identified by color contrasts that both isolate the serpentine form from appendages and identify the various other design units that compose the overall depiction and make it recognizable as a particular type of bird or beast.

The serpent is virtually ubiquitous in Coclé ceramic designs, appearing either by itself or as the foundation unit of other types of creatures. Distinctive characteristics of the serpent, including its particular pattern of markings, the duality of identical head-end and tail-end, and kennings based on serpent forms and markings, will be found to underlie the overall patterning of many ceramic designs, even when the serpent per se does not appear.

The serpent is sometimes portrayed in very straightforward terms (Fig. 3; see also Lothrop 1976:27). More frequently, however, it appears as a basic body form for other animal depictions. Fig. 4 shows an excellent and very clear-cut example and provides a number of other characteristics that can begin to sharpen our appreciation of the Coclé designs. In this design the body of the bird is clearly in the form of a serpent, complete with realistic "head-end" and extended tongue. This serpent is distinguishable from the adjacent legs and torso of the bird by color contrast; the serpent form is purple and the legs red. The design seems to imply that there is an essential serpent quality inherent in the composition of "bird," that "bird" (perhaps living as well as in design) is conceived of as basically a serpent-derived creature with definitive bird

appendages, and/or the quality of bird contains the quality of the serpent. Perhaps it is energized by serpentness.

Certain other features of this design may be noted by way of anticipating later topics. For example, this bird has three legs, two of which, rendered in two colors, are animalistic or avian in form and one of which, rendered in a single color, is human in form. The human leg parallels the serpent's tail and calls to mind the mytheme of the severed leg as a possible source of the blood that marked birds and animals with their zoologically characteristic colors (see chapter 6).

All three legs are also striped with parallel lines or ligatures. Some of these lines are contained by the outline of the leg, but the lower ligatures on the two bird legs extend beyond the outline of the leg. This is probably not accidental, for close examination of other examples of ligature depictions shows the same contrast (Figs. 5 and 63). I would suggest that when the ligatures stay within the outline of the leg, they denote a human or perhaps "cultural" context for the creature's identification, and when the ligatures extend beyond the outline of the leg, they designate an animal or "nature" context. When both modes of ligature depiction occur on the same creature, the design may encode duality or human-animal transformation.

A transformation theme may occur in other design motifs. Again with reference to Fig. 4, note how the head of the bird and the human foot (and serpent's tail) face in one direction, while the serpent's head and the bird feet face in the opposite direction. Anticipating the discussion of birds to come (chapter 3), I would suggest again the possibility of a duality and/or transformation theme involving the cultural

FIG. 5. *Female form showing contrasting modes of ligature depictions. From Lothrop (1976:25).*

FIG. 6. *Double-headed serpentine creature with distinctive oval-and-rectangle body markings characteristic of the boa constrictor. From Lothrop (1976:55).*

realm or ordered world of human society (represented by the type of bird—see below) versus the natural world in the sense of the still-unordered primordial realm (represented by the formless serpent as originator or primal creature). Another feature of this design—the particular curvilinear forms given to the serpent, the bird's head-torso, and the bird's legs, respectively—again should be noted briefly by way of anticipating later discussion. Suffice to say here that this particular form, the so-called Y-element, which is also extremely common in Coclé art, may also be designative of generalized serpent quality. This point is argued in more detail below.

Before continuing with additional examples of creatures containing serpent qualities, it is necessary to try zoologically to identify the appropriate reptile since its presence in design often is not as clearly drawn as in Figs. 3 and 4 but may be indicated instead by distinctive markings alone or by a combination of body form and markings. Fig. 6 offers a major clue to the zoological serpent in question. The design portrays a double-headed and legged creature with a long sinuous body form distinctively marked with alternating ovals and concave-sided rectangles. Although the legged creature may refer to a saurian, possibly an iguana (Helms 1977:108), the body markings are virtually identical to those of the red-tailed boa constrictor *(Constrictor constrictor* or *Boa constrictor ortonii)* shown in Fig. 7. As this figure shows, and as Fig. 8 illustrates (sketched while observing a red-tailed boa at the local science center), the characteristic body markings of the boa show a very clear repetitive pattern of ovals separated by darker, more or less rectangular patches with concave ends. On either side of this band of ovals and rectangles

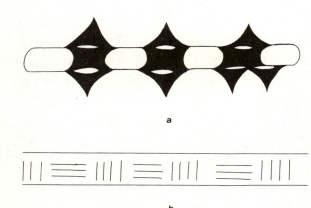

is a series of dark triangles with slightly concave bases adjacent to the top band and with points facing away.

The red-tailed boa is common in Panama, and Lothrop commented that boas "abound[ed]" in the vicinity of Sitio Conte (1942:73). The boa takes the place of the anaconda, the large aquatic constrictor of South American tropical rivers that is not present in the Panamanian isthmus, although boas do not obtain the great size and length (as much as twenty-five feet) of the anaconda (Schmidt and Inger 1957:176–177). Mature boas are generally six to nine feet long, though maximum length may reach fifteen to eighteen feet (Schmidt and Inger 1957:176; Greene 1983) and are terrestrial and good climbers rather than aquatic serpents. In addition, if the terrestrial red-tailed boa is the major serpent portrayed in the Coclé ceramics, the thematic material expressed by serpent designs may possibly contrast in significant ways with South American aquatic anaconda-based mythemes. Conceivably the Panamanian symbolism contains certain structural inversions of South American materials. For example, whereas the anaconda in native South American epistomology is associated with the realm of water and beneficent rain, the serpent in the cosmology of native peoples of the isthmus may be associated more with the realm of the terrestrial and, perhaps, with harmful rain (e.g., hurricanes, as noted above).

Lévi-Strauss has noted, in passing, that structural contrasts can be found when certain contemporary Kuna (Panama) myths dealing with the origins of cooking fire are compared to their tropical South American counterparts (1969:138, note 15). Similarly, Bozzoli de Wille and Cubero have independently recognized certain structural inversions in

FIG. 7. *Boa constrictor. From Harter (1979:180).*

FIG. 8(a). *Back and side markings of adult boa constrictor.*

FIG. 8(b). *Bar-line kennings derived from boa markings.*

Talamancan mythemes from southeastern Costa Rica when compared with northern South American myths (1988; see also chap. 6). Reichel-Dolmatoff has also observed that in the symbolism of the Colombian Tukano tribes the boa constrictor and the anaconda are strongly contrasted. Land-dwelling serpents, especially the boa and many colorful and also poisonous snakes, "symbolize a male principle, an outward-acting and aggressive force." They are opposed to the anaconda and other water-dwelling snakes, which represent a female principle and constitute "a uterine and maternal symbol" but with negative and destructive qualities and are associated with the color black. The boa, on the other hand, with its bright colors, symbolizes the joy of dancing (Reichel-Dolmatoff 1975:138–139; Reichel-Dolmatoff 1971:102–103, 164).[1]

Among the Makiritare or So'to of Venezuela, both the boa and the anaconda are female principles, but the mythic boa has solar associations as daughter of the sun, while the aquatic anaconda, as mythic Great Snake, is recognized as the mistress of water and mother of all things aquatic (de Civrieux 1980:51–54, 122, 180–181). A somewhat comparable contrast is mentioned again by Reichel-Dolmatoff in speaking of astronomical concepts held by the Tukano: "The Milky Way is imagined as two huge snakes; the starry, luminous part is a rainbow boa, a male principle, and the dark part an anaconda, a female principle" (1982:171). In short, the terrestrial boa as replacement for the aquatic anaconda in Panamanian symbolism may not only be a zoological necessity but part of a larger corpus of symbolism that contrasts structurally with at least some South American symbolic forms, even though comparable messages may be encoded.

Be that as it may, judging from body markings depicted on Fig. 6 and the ease with which this identification can be applied to other examples, as we shall see, the fundamental serpent depicted in Coclé polychrome ceramics appears to be the boa. I further suggest that the distinctive boa markings are also found, very often, in the form of a kenning[2] in which the alternating ovals and rectangles are replaced by alternating units of horizontal parallel lines and vertical parallel lines, as seen in Fig. 8(b). Fig. 3 provides an example of this design motif. Here, and in other examples that will follow, I interpret the basic body form delineated by such alternating units of parallel lines to be indicative of the presence of the boa or to stipulate that the quality of the Great Serpent was inherent in such creatures. This proposed interpretation seems supported also by the fact that horizontal bar-lines (actually irregular rows of dots) may appear in nature on some of the patches marking the boa constrictor.

Before leaving Fig. 6, the theme of duality arises once again. One of the striking features of this design is the virtually identical portrayal of the head-end and the tail-end of the basic serpent form. (The lack of a clearly appendaged head and/or tail is one of the fundamental features emphasizing the formlessness or lack of differentiating appendages characteristic of the serpent both in life and as mytheme). We see, in fact, two heads each shaped and drawn like the other but at the same time differentiated by means of color contrast: the jaws or mouth of one head-end are red, while those of the other are purple. The units constituting the crest on each of the heads are contrasted by color, too, and the portion that is red on one head is purple on the other.

The alternation of ovals and rectangles along the serpentine body is further differentiated by red versus purple color contrast, and the two legs, though not mirror opposites, show significant color patterning—one being all purple and the other half-red and half-purple. Again, themes of duality and perhaps of transformation may be suggested by this careful and deliberate use of color. The single-color purple leg and purple-jawed head may represent the "cultural" half of the duality/transformation theme, while the red-jawed head and two-toned leg may represent the "natural" half of that theme. (This interpretation is influenced also by the appearance of "chin whiskers"—perhaps an animal or "nature" motif—on the red head, and the absence thereof on the purple head).

If in fact color coding, that is to say chromatics, carries some fundamental symbolic significance in this art as, judging from the careful symmetries and patternings in its use, it seems to do, we may look again at the ovals and rectangles of the serpentine body form and ask whether ovals, all being the same color (in this case purple), express a particular quality different from that accorded to rectangles, which are all a contrasting red. Fig. 9 suggests there is a difference. The design on the bowl of the vessel appears to depict a sinuous serpent body with plain-colored rectangular panels alternating with figured rectangles out of which legged and head-crested creatures emerge. I suggest that in this figure the alternating plain and figured panels correspond to the rectangles and ovals of the boa design, respectively, and that part of this design, perhaps

FIG. 9. *Crested figures emerging from boa marking. From Lothrop (1976:58).*

the ovals-cum-figured panels, are considered to contain and/or to represent the particular generative, life-giving or life-identifying qualities of the serpent; that is, they reveal the serpent as the "source" of other life forms.

Support for this theory may be found in Fig. 10 (see also Lothrop 1976:49 top l.), which may depict a close-up of a boa oval (in this depiction a circle) flanked by portions of the adjacent boa rectangles. The oval/circle contains a bird and may represent the boa-cum-Great Serpent as generative source or origin point of the bird. Conceivably a design such as Fig. 11 (see also Lothrop 1976:9 bottom r.) portrays a comparable theme. Here the boa oval/circle alone may be represented, identified by surrounding units of parallel light red and dark red bands plus a related curvilinear kenning in rectangular panels (see below) and containing another type of creature (again common to Coclé art; see chapter 4). All of these depictions of creatures, contained within or emanating from the ovals of the serpent, may express the role of the Great Serpent as primordial source of life for various mythological and symbolically significant animal forms. These portrayals would be in general accord with myths identifying the serpent as source, by its blood, of the definitive zoological characteristics that identify given animal species and/or as source of living forms from its body.[3]

However, a more negatively structured tale from the Miskito Coast of eastern Nicaragua is interesting in this context, too. Briefly, an evil spirit that took the form of a boa stole and swallowed the wife of Thunder, who had been sent to earth by God to instruct people in agriculture and various other arts and crafts. Thunder challenged the boa

who then swallowed his own wife, too, to keep her from falling into the hands of Thunder. The two enemies then vied with each other to see who could grow tallest and reach the clouds. Thunder won and immediately killed the boa, cut him in pieces, and restored to life the people who had been swallowed. (The various parts of the boa's body turned to rocks, which, Indians claim, sometimes bleed) (Conzemius 1932:127).

Several ceramic pieces provide further examples of the various serpent-related design motifs discussed so far, including the serpent by itself (see Fig. 46 [central panel]) or the serpent as basic body form for other animals constructed as serpents-with-appendages, the use of bar-line kennings for serpent identification, and the oval-and-rectangle theme as representing serpent (boa) markings. Beginning with the latter, the end strips and central strip of Fig. 12 may depict the alternating boa oval-and-rectangle theme in kenning form. Anticipating further discussion below, it may also be remarked here that the triangular V-elements of which these designs are composed are also part of zoological boa markings, for, as Fig. 7 shows, rows of triangles flank both sides of the line of ovals and rectangles. Consider, too, Fig. 13, where the end and central strips may be understood to depict a sequence of boa ovals and concave-sided rectangles, though each oval now contains a motif that may seem to involve a limb and foot (note possible ligatures; see also severed limb discussion in chapter 6).

Other "median-strip" design motifs might well be derived from the alternating oval-rectangle units of boa markings, too, and may also encode the theme of animals contained within and/or emergent from the body of the serpent. Median strips frequently contain what appear

FIG. 12. *Crustaceans alternating with geometric strip designs suggesting alternating boa oval-and-rectangle markings. From Lothrop (1976:88).*

FIG. 13. *Crustaceans alternating with strip designs suggesting boa ovals and rectangles. Each oval contains a limb-and-foot motif. From Lothrop (1976:88).*

to be limb portions (lower limb and foot or paw) arranged in sequence, sometimes within the sinuous curve of the serpent form itself. The central panel of Fig. 14 (see also Fig. 46 [central bar]) shows a series of "limbs" in the somewhat oval spaces within the serpent's body curves, with hints in the form of Y-element kennings of the rectangular marking emerging from the serpent form at the opposite side of the curve. The entire composition suggests limbs correlating with animal forms within the ovals alternating with rectangle kennings along the length of the serpent form (see also Figs. 13 and 50). Variants occur in which the sinuous serpent form composing the median strip is depicted entirely in Y-element kennings with several clawed feet interspersed (Fig. 15) or as ovals, each of which contains a claw, alternating with rectangles, depicted as V-element kennings, without a separate serpent body form (Fig. 16; see also Lothrop 1976:41 lower r.). Alternatively, we find the limb-and-foot motif simply alternating with units of multiple vertical bars. This design may be representative of ovals with emergent animals (depicted by limb-and-foot as a kenning) alternating with rectangles as bar-units (Fig. 17; see also Fig. 93 and Lothrop 1976:88 top l.).

The serpent as basic body form is clearly indicated in many motifs, once the eye is trained to see it. On Fig. 3 the very straightforward serpent has a dark tail, strongly suggesting the distinctive dark-colored tail of the red-tailed boa. Many serpent-like forms also show one or two clawed limbs, frequently small but definitely present, suggesting a zoological identification as a saurian, perhaps a lizard or iguana, for the creature with serpent quality (Fig. 18; see also Lothrop 1976:frontispiece, 27 lower l.).

FIG. 14. *Hemispheres separated by central panel containing serpentine form with boa ovals containing foot-and-limb motif and hints of boa rectangles. From Lothrop (1976:8).*

FIG. 15. *Hemispheres separated by central panel with serpentine motif depicted by Y-element kenning and clawed appendages in lieu of boa ovals. From Lothrop (1976:15).*

FIG. 16. *Quadripartite design with central panel depicting boa ovals and rectangles stylized as clawed appendages and V-elements. From Lothrop (1976:43).*

FIG. 17. *Hemispheric designs with central panel depicting alternating boa ovals and rectangles in form of limb-and-foot motif and parallel bar-units, respectively. From Lothrop (1976:88).*

FIG. 18. *Legged creature with serpent body form. From Lothrop (1976:103).*

FIG. 19. *Anteater with serpentine body form. From Lothrop (1976:55).*

Fig. 18 also portrays the serpent-like saurian with two long protrusions emanating from its chin. These bring to mind a Talamancan myth telling how Sibu, the creator, constructed the sky as his home. In the process he needed a vine to tie the house together (as traditional Talamancan houses are constructed). Lacking such a vine, he turned instead to a large serpent with great whiskers who dwelt in the east where the sun rises. He sent a group of men to the serpent to pull out a whisker (it was so large it took twenty-five men to roll it up and carry it to Sibu), and used it to tie his house (Stone 1962:55). Conceivably, such a whiskered serpent is indicated in the Coclé ceramics in Fig. 18. (See also Fig. 88 and possibly 39; Lothrop 1976:frontispiece, 19 top l., 19 top r., possibly 18 top l., 26 top l., 26 lower r., 26 center r., and the abstract or kenning design of 20 top r., 8 top r., and 9 top r.).

Returning to the serpent as basic body form in design motifs, Fig. 20 portrays a mammalian creature, perhaps a tapir, whose basic body form is shown, by color contrast, to be serpentine. Similarly, Fig. 19 portrays a four-footed animal with a long snout whose basic body form, differentiated by color, is distinctly serpentine. Judging by the round mammalian ears, long strands of fur on the back, and protruding vermiform tongue, the creature depicted may be an anteater.

Anteaters are frequently found in South American myths in a variety of generally negative contexts (though powerful they are also greedy, solitary, non- or anti-social). Sometimes they stand as rival or opposite for the jaguar; sometimes they appear to have symbolic attributes opposite those of the serpent. For example, anteaters eat ants,

which are associated with the dry earth of ant heaps that for Lévi-Strauss signifies nature as opposed to the moistness of potters' clay, associated with culture and with the rainbow-cum-serpent. In Brazilian folklore, the anteater sometimes acts in a constrictor-like fashion by suffocating the jaguar with its front legs (Lévi-Strauss 1969:190). The anteater is also said to be a creature with no mouth and no anus (the mouth and anus are closed or "blocked"), which again seems to contrast it with the serpent whose head-end "equals," or is identical to, its tail-end in a more "positive" sense, in that when the serpent's two extremities are portrayed as heads in Coclé art the mouths are open rather than closed or "blocked" (Lévi-Strauss 1969:189–191, 248; Lévi-Strauss 1973:135, 61–66, 357n; Lévi-Strauss 1988:98–100).

In many other designs the presence of the fundamental serpentine body form is evidenced by sets of parallel horizontal and vertical bars within the body of the creature depicted. Fig. 21 (see also Lothrop 1976:90 bottom), for example, depicts such kennings in the basic torso of the creature. (In addition, the "streamers" emanating from each eye on Fig. 21 are suggestive of the postorbital stripe that is found on each side of the boa head and may be another way of identifying the serpentine nature of the creature depicted.) Here again, although the creature appears strongly serpentine (but note the single leg suggesting a saurian identity zoologically—see Helms 1977:109–111), a distinction or dualism is shown by means of color contrast as well as with bar-line units between the fundamental serpent quality of the creature (red) and its distinctive animal form (purple). In Fig. 22 the serpentine tail of the

FIG. 20. *Tapir with serpentine body form. From Lothrop (1976:43).*

FIG. 21. *Legged serpentine creature with serpent quality indicated by color contrast and alternating units of vertical and horizontal bar-line kennings. From Lothrop (1976:41).*

FIG. 22. *Sloth-like monkey, or mythological tailed sloth, with serpent quality indicated by alternating units of vertical and horizontal bar-line kennings in tail. From Lothrop (1976:46).*

FIG. 23. *Iguana with serpent quality indicated by alternating units of vertical and horizontal bar-line kennings in serpentine body form. From Lothrop (1976:22).*

FIG. 24. *Creature imbued with serpent quality as indicated by vertical and horizontal bar-line kennings in torso and legs. From Lothrop (1976:23).*

FIG. 25. *Curassow-like birds imbued with serpent quality as indicated by bar-line kennings in body form. From Lothrop (1976:11).*

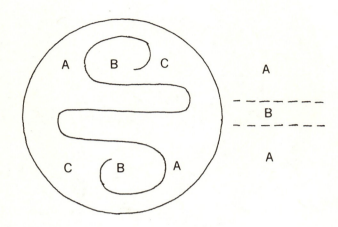

sloth–like (long curved claws, long strands of fur on legs, general facial depiction) creature is marked with boa bar-lines (see chapter 4 regarding sloths; Pressman 1991:84 describes how a mythological sloth that once had a tail lost it. The blood of that severed tail provided coloration for birds).

Fig. 23 indicates, again with bar-lines, that the essential body form or internal essence or quality of this iguana (the distinctive thick tongue is a characteristic iguana trait both in myths and in nature; Helms 1977:69) is serpentine. Serpent bar-lines need not be numerous to make the point. Fig. 24 contains only a few bar-lines in the torso and legs of the beast, but this is sufficient to establish the presence of essential serpent quality, as do the few lines in the body of the jaunty crested birds in Fig. 25.

The theme of the serpent is also expressed in the frequent depiction of identical head-endedness and tail-endedness that presumably refers to the similarity between the tapering head-end and tapering tail-end of the serpent form in nature. This motif is often portrayed by depiction of two heads, one at each end of a central body form (instead of a head and a tail), signaling that head equals tail. Fig. 6 (see also Fig. 39), the boa-bodied form discussed above, clearly portrays this, although color contrast indicates that the two head-ends are not exactly identical. Fig. 26 shows a double-headed serpentine form in which, again, the serpentine quality is color contrasted (light red) with the dark red heads of the parrot (note dark red wings flanking each side of the heads). Alternatively the birds in question may be quetzals. Fig. 27 associates much the same head shape (indication of a slight crest suggests the quetzal's slightly

FIG. 26(a). *Double-headed serpent form with parrot or quetzal heads depicting similarity of serpent head-end and tail-end in nature. From Lothrop (1976:23).*

FIG. 26(b). *Schematic detail of design elements in Fig. 26(a).*

FIG. 27. *Quetzal with long, serpentine tail feather. From Lothrop (1976:89).*

FIG. 28(a). *Serpent head-end/tail-end duality expressed with color-contrasted abstract design and Y-element kennings representing animal kennings. From Lothrop (1976:58).*

bushy crest) with what could easily be a quetzel's long ("serpent-like") tail.[4] It is particularly interesting in this context to find a Talamancan (Bribri) myth in which a huge snake transforms into a quetzel when shot by a hunter (Guevara-Berger 1993:373). Of course, zoological features of both the parrot and the quetzal could be expressed in a design format relating the symbolism of a particular category of bird that included both zoological forms to basic serpent quality.

Once the basic idea of serpentine double-headedness or head-end/tail-end duality is grasped, this motif can readily be found even in highly formalized, seemingly abstract designs. Fig. 28, for example, shows a double-ended design in which the color coding is reversed for each "end." This design motif is also noteworthy because it can be understood to portray several double-ended motifs if the Y-element kenning at the end of the circular line leading from each color-coded "head" (and/or "tail") is also regarded as a head- (or tail-) end. See Fig. 28(b) A and B; see also Fig. 38.

To appreciate this point (and the subtlety of such design) it is necessary to consider further how the serpent may be encoded in the V- or Y-element kenning, a very widely used, possibly "redundant" or "key" symbol in Coclé ceramic designs (Bateson 1972:147–148). The design motifs on Coclé polychrome ceramics abound in the use of the so-called V-element or Y-element or sometimes YC scroll motifs, the latter being identical to the former except for the addition of a long, usually curvilinear tail (Fig. 29) (Linares 1977:46–50; Lothrop 1942: 15–22). I suggest that this very widely used set of motifs served as ken-

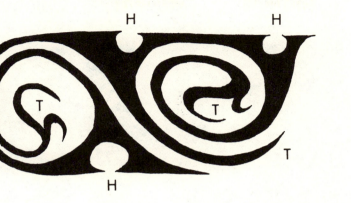

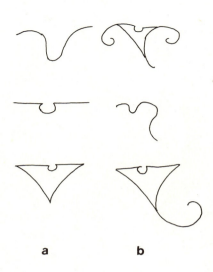

a   b

FIG. 28(b). *Schematic detail of multiple Y-elements as kennings for animal forms in Figure 28(a). H=head-end; T=tail-end.*

FIG. 29. *V-element and Y-element design motifs. a=V-element; b=Y-element.*

FIG. 30(a). *Y-element motif compared with coiled serpent form.*

nings to express the quality of the serpent for viewers who understood the intended allusion.[5]

This identification of Y- and V-elements as serpent kennings also rests on several additional observations. As Fig. 30(a) shows, the Y-element corresponds closely to the coil pattern frequently assumed by heavy-bodied constrictors (see Fig. 7; also Helms 1993b:226, Figs. 7.7 and 7.8). In addition, Greene (1983:381) comments that boas, when aggressive, "sometimes hiss loudly with the mouth partly opened and draw the head and neck into an S-shaped posture. ..."[6] The V-element is also clearly delineated in the distinctive side markings on red-tailed boa constrictors where rows of triangular V-element designs parallel both sides of the oval-rectangle units along the length of the snake's body. This can be seen in Figs. 7 and 8(a).

It is interesting, too, that rows of triangular markings along the sides of the body are characteristic of the bushmaster (*Lachesia muta*), a very large (up to twelve feet) pit viper common to the isthmus (Schmidt and Inger 1957:270). Bushmaster triangles also contain an interior dark spot, and Y-element designs with an interior spot or "eye" sometimes occur in Coclé designs (Figs. 17, 31, and 33; see also rim pattern on Lothrop 1976:108 lower l.) In a detail (Fig. 32) from Lothrop 1976:41 lower r. the "eye" in the double-Y-element crescent is portrayed as a distinct serpent-like motif, and the dark streak connecting the animal eye to the Y-element suggests the characteristic postorbital bar or streak that runs across and behind the eye on the boa head (Fig. 7). It is intriguing also to note the similarity between the shape of the constellation Scorpius,

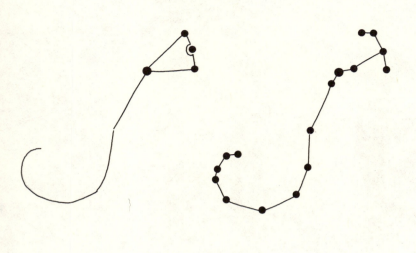

FIG. 30(b). *Y-element motif compared with constellation Scorpius.*

FIG. 31. *Double Y-element crescent motif with center "eye" suggestive of bushmaster markings. From Lothrop (1976:104).*

FIG. 32. *Detail from Lothrop (1976:41 lower r.) showing double Y-element crescent motif with emergent serpent form as central "eye."*

widely associated with the Great Snake in Amazonian beliefs, and the Coclé Y-element, including the "eye" (Fig. 30(b)) (Lévi-Strauss 1969:232, Fig. 15; Freidel, Schele, and Parker 1993:103, Fig. 2.33; Barton and Barton 1943:32).

Finally, Richard Cooke suggests a correlation between the multi-colored banded rim on plates in the Coclé Macaracas style and the coral snake (Cooke 1985:39; see also Schrimpff 1989:100). It is entirely conceivable that all these zoological species are included in the various design motifs expressing the symbolism of the "serpent" in Coclé art, although, judging by design forms on the Sitio Conte polychromes and considering the fundamental role of constrictors in indigenous cosmologies, the boa constrictor seems to hold primacy as zoological manifestation of the isthmian version of the Great Snake or rainbow serpent.[7]

Considering how V-elements and Y-elements are depicted on the Coclé ceramics, it would appear that the tail of the Y-element corresponds to a serpent tail and the triangular portion of the Y- or V-element corresponds to a serpent head. Considered in this light, a design such as Fig. 33 depicts on the bowl of the vessel, in which the tail of the Y-element becomes a creature's head, can be interpreted as a variation on the double-headed serpent theme, the V-portion of the design serving as a geometrized (kenning motif) head-end conjoined to the "other" head by the serpent body form (note parallel boa bars on body). The central panel in Fig. 34(a), which clearly shows, with color contrast, a sinuous serpent body with elaborate curvilinear V- and Y-elements attached, can be understood to depict the quality of the serpent with

even greater impact since each end of the snake is elaborated into a V-element "head," and Y-elements erupt along the length of the body, suggesting the emergence of creatures from the ovals of the serpent as seen above in Fig. 9(a).

The ubiquity of V- and Y-elements, and thus the ubiquity of the quality of serpentness as basic to the form and dynamics of living things, is also indicated in the shape given to the body parts and over-all form of many of the creatures portrayed in Coclé ceramic art. Flowing V- and Y-elements are frequently incorporated into design forms, either singly or in multiples, to depict body lines, mouths, head crests, legs, and the like. Like the bar-line kennings, this mode of design formation seems to associate animal forms with an inherent quality of serpentness, suggesting that creatures of all sorts (mammals, birds, reptiles), regardless of extraneous appendages, are basically or essentially composed of the quality of serpentness.

For example, the elegant fluid lines composing the creature in Fig. 35 (see also Fig. 23) (perhaps an iguana, if the broad tongue is taken as diagnostic of this animal's zoological identity) are basically a series of V- and Y-elements composing basic body form, open mouth, tongue, head crest, and the shape of each leg. In Fig. 4 the jaunty bird with the severed leg becomes a composition in Y-elements, illustrated in Fig. 37(a). Similarly, Fig. 36, which appears to be another anteater, combines a series of V-elements to create the central body shape as well as leg shape and "filler" motif above and below, while the anteater's tongue is a definite Y-element, illustrated in Fig. 37(c).

FIG. 33(a). Y-element design on bowl panel in which the tail of the legged creature is also the tail of a Y-element, creating a "double-headed" design format. From Lothrop (1976:56).

FIG. 33(b). Detail of Fig. 33(a).

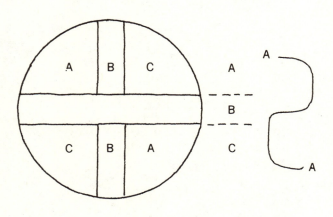

FIG. 34(a). *Quadripartite plate with central panel depicting (by color contrast) serpentine form with serpentine Y-elements elaborating head-/tail-ends. Y-elements also create serpent ovals and "emerge" from the ovals. From Lothrop (1976:10).*

FIG. 34(b). *Schematic detail of design elements in Fig. 34(a).*

FIG. 35. *Iguana design composed of serpentine Y-elements. From Lothrop (1976:16).*

FIG. 36. *Anteater design composed of serpentine V-elements and Y-elements. From Lothrop (1976:69).*

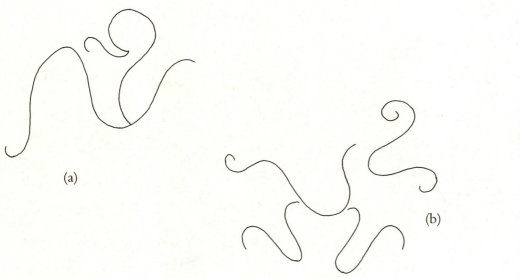

(b)

(c)

FIG. 37. *Use of Y-elements and V-elements in design construction of Figs. 4, 23, and 36.*

In like fashion, Fig. 38 appears as an elegant and sophisticated rendition of two animals in the form of Y-elements, the head of each in stylized V-shape and the tail of each becoming a colorized body form with what seems to be a claw attached.

Applying concepts suggested about color contrast, V- and Y-elements, and double-headed images, it becomes possible to begin to decode, at least in a general way, what otherwise appear to be very abstract curvilinear designs. For example, Fig. 14 can now be seen as a variant of Fig. 39 in which two red Y-elements corresponding to the side heads in Fig. 39 flank a central blue/black "face" composed of Y-elements. Each of the V- or Y-elements of the side or flanking "heads" in Fig. 14 also ends in a color-contrasted "tail," suggesting an additional head-end/tail-end comparability.

Furthermore, if the design of Fig. 14 is closely studied, small "tear-drop" eyes are seen along the edges of the design within the indentation formed by the Y-elements forming the edge. These eyes, together with the color content of the "tail-ends" of the respective Y-elements, suggest that the multivocality of the design is meant to include a series of creatures positioned along the edges. (Alternatively it is possible that the "tail-ends" identified by color contrast for all these creatures are meant to be head crests. See below regarding the comparability of appendages as suggested by color coding).

In a simpler exercise, the top and bottom hemispheres of Fig. 40 can each be understood both as a serpent body form (color contrasted) with both ends flaring into Y-element designs (head-end and tail-end as heads) and as a full-frontal view of two heads facing each other below

FIG. 38. *Abstract depiction, using V- and Y-elements, of two animals, each composed of a Y-element with a head (V-element) joined to a colorized body (Y-element tail) and claw. From Lothrop (1976:45).*

FIG. 39. *Hemispheric designs composed of Y-elements creating legged, double-headed serpentine creatures flanking a central face. From Lothrop (1976:8).*

FIG. 40. *Abstract hemispheric designs each composed of serpentine Y-elements constituting a central colorized body form flanked by Y-elements simultaneously facing each other as head-ends and composing head-/tail-end similarity for the central body form. From Lothrop (1976:4).*

FIG. 41. *Crustacean, perhaps in boa oval, encircled by Y-elements composing multiple serpentine forms interlinked by head-/tail-end similarities. From Lothrop (1976:4).*

the serpent form, both heads created by the two Y-elements that seem to face each other in a manner suggestive of Fig. 39. Similarly, a design such as Fig. 41 may tentatively be interpreted as a sea creature (lobster or crab) surrounded by multiple series of Y-element head-ends and tail-ends indicative of a series of encircling serpents or of an encircling quality of serpentness. It is tempting to suggest that the circle in which the creature is placed corresponds to a boa oval and that the overall design concerns the serpent as mythical source or origin (from its body) of this type of sea creature. Alternatively, chapter 5 discusses the mythical World Tree as source of sea animals, in which case the serpents in Fig. 41 may be surrounding the tree depicted in cross-section. In Fig. 42, if color coding is considered, the central circle (the boa oval?) is surrounded by several double-ended serpents with the (head–) end of one serpent becoming the (tail–) end of the adjacent one. Note that the color of the serpent bodies is the same as the central circle/oval, suggesting that the circle may be a cross-section of the serpent.

FIG. 42. *Central circle (boa oval or body cross-section?) surrounded by double-headed serpents linked by interlocking head-/tail-ends. From Lothrop (1976:28).*

3   BIRDS AND FOWL

Some of the most engaging design motifs on the Coclé polychromes depict birds. Here again, as with the serpent motif, at least some of the information coded in these designs may be revealed by the particular zoological species chosen for depiction. Consequently, zoological identification may serve as a first step in interpreting these design motifs, although it also seems reasonable to assume that birds as symbolic motifs are not necessarily depicted in truly naturalistic form. Nonetheless, I also assume methodologically that at least some small clue to the intended zoological correlate is usually provided for the creatures portrayed.

Many of the Coclé birds are posed as seemingly terrestrial creatures energetically stepping out in more or less full stride. This apparent terrestrial (rather than volant) posture seems to parallel the terrestrial preference discerned in other thematic and stylistic Coclé design contexts, such as the replacement of the aquatic anaconda by the terrestrial boa discussed above. It is also evidenced in the frequent portrayals, both in metal work and in painted designs, of legged saurians (Helms 1977).

In addition to their frequent portrayal as dynamic walkers, the modes of depiction of Coclé birds suggest at least two further typological categories. The first depicts a bird frequently sporting a head crest or head appendage and a long barred tail. Portrayals of this birds also indicate a serpent body form and often (but not always) a posture in which the head is turned backward, looking over the shoulder towards the tail. The second type of bird has a shorter body form characterized by a rounded rump and no tail or only faintly delineated tail. It is portrayed as forward-looking with no evidence of the serpent motif, and a long, very

obvious wattle depends from the neck. I suggest that these two categories of birds are based upon two distinct zoological-cosmological prototypes that address a common issue but with different referential markers. The first category may portray one or more species of curassow portrayed as the primordial formless serpent-with-appendages. The second category may also conceptualize the attainment of form or order out of formlessness as expressed by the addition of appendages to another primordially formless creature, the tinamou. The tinamou-plus-appendages that is then depicted may be tentatively identified either as the wild turkey or as one or more species of guan.

Figs. 43 and 44 (see also Figs. 46 and 25; Lothrop 1976:9 l.) show the energetic bird of the first category. In these depictions a long, barred tail is made markedly distinct, by color contrast, from the serpentine body form which, in some examples, is identified by boa bars or, in the case of Fig. 43, by a sequence of concave ovals. These birds also sport a head crest, some more elaborate than others. In Fig. 43 (see also Lothrop 1976:7 lower r.) the bird faces forward while in Fig. 44 and other examples in Lothrop (1976) the bird faces backward.

The definitive clues to the zoological identification of this bird may be the barred tail, backward-turned head, distinct head crest and terrestrial locomotion. These characteristics suggest either a cracid, such as the great curassow (*Crax rubra*), or possibly (if the seemingly terrestrial character of these depictions is down-played) a raptor, perhaps the harpy eagle (*Harpia harpyja*), the crested eagle (*Morphnus guianensis*), or the ornate hawk eagle (*Spizaetus ornatus*). All of these large, powerful raptors have long, markedly barred tails and distinctive head crests (Ridgely and Gwynne 1989:103–106; Wetmore 1965:241–251) but are not strongly terrestrial in either zoological habits or mythological symbolism. Indeed, in the gold work of ancient Panama, when eagles or comparable birds of prey are depicted, they characteristically appear in frontal pose with spread wings and broad tail.[1]

The eagle is, however, on a par with the serpent as a major primordial creature in native American myths. Eagle-shaman transformation is common (Furst 1991:106–107), and the association of the eagle with other forms of political leadership is common, too; the golden eagles worn as part of chiefly regalia in the pre-Columbian Intermediate Area is a case in point. The eagle is also implicated in myths concerning the original coloring of birds. In some tales eagle blood (like serpent blood) produced such coloration (Pressman 1991:85), or an eagle killed the terrapin whose bloodied body produced bird colors (Lévi-Strauss 1969:317) or severed the leg of the boy whose blood produced pots full of paint with which the various birds were colored (Pressman 1991:85). It is interesting to note, too, that the eagle is associated with success in hunting by Kuna Indians, who allegedly use shavings from preserved eagle heads in concoctions of hunting medicine (Wassén 1965:28).

For all these reasons, the eagle cannot be dismissed as a possible zoological prototype for the Coclé bird motif in question. However, I would like to consider another zoological candidate, the great curassow, whose behavioral and physiological characteristics also fit the depictions very well, perhaps better than the eagle.

The great curassow is a very large, graceful gallinaceous ("turkey-like") bird with heavy body, small head with a prominent curly head crest, rounded wings, long powerful legs, and elongated tail (Fig. 45). In females the tail is distinctively banded. This bird is found in rain forests and woodlands of tropical America, including Panama, and while generally a tree inhabitant, it spends considerable time on the ground feeding on fallen fruit. Like other cracids, the great curassow also has the habit of passing the head back over the shoulder and wings in a kind of false preening (Ridgely and Gwynne 1989:113, 115; Delacour and Amadon 1973:6, 10, 13, 73, 211–215; Wetmore 1965:293–298).

Cracids in general are also characterized by colorful wattles, horns, knobs, and patches of skin on face or throat, and some have brightly colored legs and feet. They evidence an association with clay, too, in that

FIG. 45. *The great curassow (Crax rubra). Note knob on forehead of male and distinctive banding on tail of female. Based on Ridgely and Gwynne (1989:Plate 41, no. 7).*

they have been reported sometimes to seek mineral supplements to their diets by eating a type of clayish soil. Occasionally specimens have been found with stomachs full of reddish clay and with traces of clay clinging to the beak (Delacour and Amadon 1973:12, 30). These characteristics and habits (as well as a number of others that could make them behaviorally attractive to humans)[2] could readily mark the curassow and other cracids as appropriate symbolic signifiers for chromatic-related themes.

It should be noted, too, that in the South American myths analyzed by Lévi-Strauss the curassow may be associated with the origins of cooking fire. This theme is structurally related to pottery-making and perhaps reflects an alleged attraction to fire noted for certain guans, by which means they reportedly can be lured (Bertin et al. 1980:393). In myths the curassow is also accorded symbolic significance as a distinctly terrestrial as opposed to a sky bird (birds of prey) and, like a number of other birds, acquired its unique coloration from the remains of the rainbow snake or comparable sources (Lévi-Strauss 1969:73, 75, 302, 313; Lévi-Strauss 1973:119). Curassows, like other cracids, are also distinctive for the unfailing regularity of their booming call at dawn or, for some species, at night, at such regular intervals that they are described as a kind of forest clock, a characteristic which can also recommend them for symbolism and metaphor (Delacour and Amadon 1973:12–13; Lévi-Strauss 1969:204, note 3; Lévi-Strauss 1973:280).

With these basic points in mind, let us consider in more detail some of the Coclé designs depicting these birds. When the tails, head crests and legs of the "curassow"-derived design motifs are examined more

closely, certain interesting correspondences appear. On Fig. 46, for example, the head crest takes the form of another creature indicated by a head and a leg with ligatures. The double-headed theme also appears since the bird's own head forms one "end" of the crest, and the other head is portrayed at the opposite end of the crest. In Fig. 44 the head crest of the bird on the right is simply expressed in the form of what may be a leg (note knee bend) with ligatures, paralleling in color and in ligatures the bird's own leg. In Fig. 43 (see also Fig. 25) the tail of the bird is marked with ligatures and in its straight shape is not unlike the leg-as-head-crest seen in Fig. 44. On Fig. 25 the tail and the head crest are related by color coding and are both marked with ligatures. They are identical in shape to the tail-as-leg and crest-as-leg seen in Figs. 43 and 44. There are other variations, too: in Fig. 57 the tail and head crest are identical but are banded with curassow tail stripes.

Considered overall, the "curassow" motif seems not only to encode a correlation or interchangeability (substitution pattern) between tail and head crest but also relates both to what may be the severed-leg theme first noted above on Fig. 4, where the leg with its ligatures parallels the serpent's tail. If Fig. 4 is a variation on the curassow motif, as seems likely, the severed leg in that depiction corresponds to the curassow's tail.

Before leaving the severed leg in this context (it will be considered further below), it should be noted, especially in light of the possibility that the bird depicted is zoologically an eagle, that the severed-leg motif appears in Mesoamerican myth and pictorial symbolism in the context of Huitzilopochtli–Tezcatlipoca's deformed foot or missing leg or foot,

FIG. 46. *Backward-facing cracid-like bird, perhaps modeled upon the great curassow (note banded tail). Serpentine head crest ends in the form of a separate creature, creating a double-headed motif. In central panel note serpentine form with ovals (containing leg-and-foot motifs) and hint of rectangles created by Y-element. From Lothrop (1976:10).*

FIG. 47. *Egg-laying bird probably representing the tinamou. Note serpentine Y-element within body cavity. From Lothrop (1976:58).*

and that Huitzilopochtli is associated with and/or mythically transforms into the eagle (e.g., Hunt 1977:59–60, 240–242). Furthermore, the missing foot "was the symbol of things that coil around themselves in a spiral motion" like hurricanes and whirlwinds and waterspouts that seem to "walk" across the landscape (ibid.:242). These associations clearly relate in Coclé ceramic design not only to the presence of the severed leg, which carried, as we have seen, association with color chromatics in tropical American lore, but also to both the serpent motif (apropos of things that coil) and the theme of dangerous rain (hurricanes) that may be the isthmian context of the rainbow serpent theme.

Returning to the Coclé designs, Figs. 4, 25, and 43 show a small protuberance on the forehead of the bird. Cracids in general are characterized by a variety of very colorful (in the great curassow, bright yellow) knobs or tubercles above the bill (and sometimes dewlaps below the bill) or horny projections on the skull (see Delacour and Amadon 1973:30–35, Fig. 10). Depictions of protuberances thus strengthen the argument that this design motif is based on the Cracidae, notably the curassow.

Let us turn now to a second type of bird depicted on the Coclé polychromes. Fig. 47 shows a small-headed, slender-necked bird with a rounded body form and only the smallest hint of a tail. The most notable characteristic of this bird is the clear evidence that it is laying an egg. The bird's body also shows, seemingly as indication of internal bodily processes, a serpentine Y-element positioned so as to be the "organ" responsible for the production of the egg (see also Lothrop

1976:104 top l. for similar Y-element depiction of the internal "work-ings" of a deer; Fig. 24 where the internal serpent element is depicted with bar-line kennings).[3]

Two possibilities come to mind concerning the zoological referent or prototype for this motif: a heron or a tinamou. The heron is suggested by the long neck and elongated bill plus the long body "feathers" indi-cated for head and back. Heron are sometimes significant in symbolic context because they are shore waders, frequenting the littoral between land and water. Being at home in a liminal or transitional zone between two major cosmological realms, shore birds themselves may come to sig-nify liminality and transformation, as in ancient Maya iconography (Schele and Freidel 1990:417; Schele and Miller 1986:55). Since the bird in Fig. 47 is shown as an egg-layer, however, the production of eggs must be of particular significance for the creature depicted. Herons do not seem to have any exceptional qualities, either mythical or natural, as egg-layers, but another bird—the tinamou—does.

The tinamou, especially the great tinamou (*Tinamus major*), is another distinctly terrestrial inhabitant of neotropical forest, woodland and brushy areas. Tinamous are shy and furtive birds that seek the cover of ground vegetation and are seldom seen. They have compact, chunky bodies, small heads, relatively long and slender necks, short rounded wings and very short tails (Fig. 48). On a subspecies of tinamou in east-ern Panama the feathers on the back of the head are elongated to form a small crest (Ridgely and Gwynne 1989:51; Hilty and Brown 1986:41; Wetmore 1965:5–14). The tinamou is particularly distinguished by the great beauty of both its song and its colorful eggs, the latter said to look like burnished metal or glazed porcelain and to be among the most strikingly beautiful of all birds' eggs (Bertin 1980:359). The smooth, almost enamel-like shells may appear brilliantly and intensely blue or glossy blue-green or lavender and are highly visible when laid on the dark forest floor between buttresses of large trees or perhaps at the base of a log or a clump of ferns (Ridgely and Gwynne 1989:51–52; Skutch 1983:3–7, 10; Wetmore 1965:5–14; Lancaster 1983).

In myths of the Makiritare or So'to of Venezuela the tinamou's eggs are the sole containers from which a hallucinogenic preparation (made from Banisteriopsis and elsewhere known as yagé or ayahuasca) is drunk in the "Sky Place" or Heaven (de Civrieux 1980:180). Among the Desana, where color expresses vital energies, the tinamou's capacity to

FIG. 48. *The great tinamou* (Tinamus major). *From Wetmore (1965: Fig. 2). Courtesy of the Smithsonian Institution Press.*

lay brilliantly colored eggs is also accorded very fundamental cosmological import. As Reichel-Dolmatoff explains, in the beginning of time, during the great World Fire, the tinamou hid in a gourd vessel and was thereby saved from destruction. "The reason why Tinamou was the only survivor of the World Fire lies in the fact that this bird lays remarkably brilliant-shelled eggs of many different colors and hues; it thus saved the color energies from destruction" (1978a:280).[4]

By being the creator or preserver of color chromatics, the tinamou would seem to be associated with cosmological qualities as basic as those associated with serpentness. There are other fundamental cosmological qualities associated with this bird, too. Like curassows, tinamous may convey liminality in the symbolic world because their plaintive, mournful whistle, a single long-drawn-out note with sometimes a "dip" in the middle, is heard with clock-like regularity at dawn and dusk, the transitional time between day and night, light and dark. Like its eggs, the call of the tinamou is considered a zoological marvel, "one of the most haunting and beautiful sounds of the neotropics" (Hilty and Brown 1986:42; Lancaster 1983:572). Consequently, in South American myths the tinamou, along with the curassow, is often associated with the coming of dawn, that is, with the origin, the creation, of light (Lévi-Strauss 1973:417).

In addition to being a creator or preserver of color energies and/or of light, the tinamou is also recognized in some myths as the Mother of Birds. In a Warao tale, for example, the tinamou as Mother of Birds was created as such when a hero-hunter's severed leg sprang to life as a tinamou (Lévi-Strauss 1969:110, 203–204). Elsewhere, in the Guianas, native lore speaks of a constellation identified as being in the shape of a severed leg, which is greeted with calls by tinamous when it appears on the horizon before dawn (Lévi-Strauss 1973:280; Lévi-Strauss 1969:225).[5] In the first section of this work it was noted that one of the possible sources of the coloration of birds and animals other than the rainbow snake was the blood from a severed leg. The tinamou, like the rainbow snake, thus seems identifiable as a mythical source of, or metaphor for, the identifying (organizing) coloration encoded in birds' appearances or as creator or preserver of the qualities or energies inherent in light and color.

Pursuing this idea of the tinamou as a symbolic *fons et origo*, certain other characteristics of this bird come to mind. The tinamou (sometimes called *inhambu*) has exceptionally white and very delicious meat and is thought by some natives of South America to be bloodless and hence valuable in various ritual contexts (Campbell 1989:132, 134). For the Desana, the tinamou is regarded as a yellow creature and therefore as a solar animal (correlating with the tinamou's association with the origins of light). It is also symbolic of the beautiful and the good: "the Sun itself considered it as the most perfect achievement of his Creation. It represents gentleness and aesthetic beauty. Its meat is 'pure' food" (Reichel-Dolmatoff 1971:102). Tinamous may be kept quartered in Desana villages as a personification of the good life and of good health, their meat being considered beneficial to the sick (Reichel-Dolmatoff 1971:187). The Kuna of Panama also keep tinamous, like curassows, partially domesticated (Bennett 1968:49).[6]

Not only is the tinamou regarded as bloodless (i.e., white, colorless, or the sum of all colors), but it may also be accorded the fundamental feature of formlessness comparable to that associated with the appendageless rainbow snake and other shapeless things that produced original colors or color energies for birds and animals when in a battered or formless condition (e.g., the cut-up rainbow snake, the demolished terrapin, battered humans). This brownish olive or greyish olive bird is very plain and drab, although it does have dark narrow bars on back and wings. Its tail and wings are very short, and it is entirely devoid of any really distinctive coloration or body markings. Except for the eastern Panamanian subspecies, it lacks head crests or other bodily elaborations (Campbell and Lack 1985:594; Wetmore 1965:7, Fig. 2; Hilty and Brown 1986:Plate I).

Indeed, the tinamou in appearance is as close to "generic bird" as one would wish. It is conceivable that just as the serpent "becomes" other animals when distinctive appendages, colors and sounds are added to its formless length, as Coclé designs show, so the tinamou, the Mother of Birds, may "become" other birds or may form the basis for other birds not only as layer of colorful eggs but when distinctive tails or head crests, knobs or wattles, colors or calls are added to its basic form. From this perspective, Coclé depictions of birds, such as the proposed curassow and others discussed below, might be considered as portrayals of a basic large-bodied, small-headed, thin-necked bird with various appendages—head crests, distinctive tails, wattles, etc.—added to provide specific identification of a particular type of bird.

FIG. 49. *Round-rumped, thin-necked birds possibly based on the tinamou. From Lothrop (1976:93).*

FIG. 50. *Quadripartite design featuring round-rumped, thin-necked birds with long wattle at base of throat, possibly based on the wattled guan. From Lothrop (1976:45).*

In this respect, as well as from the contexts suggested in myths, the tinamou can be compared with the serpent as a fundamental and primordial "formless" creature that serves as the originating "source" of more "ordered" (that is, appendaged) life forms.

If the very fundamental or primordial natural-cum-cosmological qualities of the tinamou—its generic "shapelessness," its association with the origins of light, its preservation of color energies, and its ability to create colorful life-giving eggs—place this bird in a thematic category comparable to that of the serpent as primordial creator/creature, it is not surprising to find that certain Coclé design motifs seem to depict other birds as basic or primordial tinamou-plus-appendages, just as various birds and animals appear to be composed of basic or primordial serpent-with-appendages.

The birds that may be associated with the tinamou are also portrayed with small heads, thin necks, stubby and round-rumped bodies, and no tail, or a tail indicated only with a dotted line. A few of the portrayals show a bird with no exceptional physical characteristics at all and may be depictions of the tinamou itself, although no egg-laying abilities are shown (Fig. 49; see also Lothrop 1976:50 top r.). The feathering suggestive of a heron in Fig. 47 may be intended to relate the heron to basic tinamou qualities, especially since heron also lay (pale) blue-green eggs. If so, the heron in question could be the Great Blue (*Ardea herodias*) or the Cocoi (also known as White-Necked, *Ardea cocoi*), both of which have long occipital plumes (Ridgely and Gwynne 1989:68, 69, Plate 1). Most designs, however, depict a bird characterized most notably by what appears to be a long wattle at the base of the throat or neck (Figs.

10 and 50). These birds may also have a long tail, indicated very unobstrusively by a curled line (Figs. 51 [top l. and lower r. quadrants] and 52 [top r. and lower l. quadrants]). In contrast to the "curassow" depictions, none of these birds carries a distinctive head crest (though head feathers, perhaps, are always indicated with a few lines) and none contains serpent bar-lines or other serpent indications. Occasionally a few short lines or excrescences are placed on the upper bill together with another set of short lines or excrescence above the bill or the forehead (Figs. 50, 51, and 52).

In the zoological realm a round-bodied terrestrial bird with a long, dangling wattle and perhaps a reasonable length of tail limits the field to very few possibilities. The wild turkey comes to mind since the turkey shows a tuft of long hair-like feathers dependent from the breast as a beard or "pectoral appendage" (Schorger 1966:80, frontispiece). However, it is not entirely clear whether the pre-Columbian range of the turkey, either wild or domesticated, had extended south beyond Costa Rica (it was well known in Mesoamerica). Many of the large, turkey-like fowl of Central America and northern South America frequently described by early Europeans undoubtedly were curassows and guans, though there is limited documentary evidence suggesting the possibility of turkeys (Schorger 1966:9; Sauer 1966:274–275; Gilmore 1950:393). How early turkeys may have arrived (assuming that if they were, they were introduced from Mesoamerica to the north) remains an open question.[7]

The other bird that fits the design motif is the wattled guan. Here, too, there is a question of range, for the wattled guan (*Aburria aburri*) is

FIG. 51. *Quadripartite design with top left and lower right quadrants featuring a full-bodied bird with hint of a tail and forehead spike, possibly based on a variety of guan. From Lothrop (1976:11).*

FIG. 52. *Depiction of full-bodied, tailed, thin-necked birds each with wattle at the base of the neck, possibly based upon the wattled guan. From Lothrop (1976:11).*

FIG. 53. *Wattled guan* (Aburria aburri). *From Delacour and Amadon (1973:33, Fig. 10 bottom r.). By permission of Albert Earl Gilbert.*

not currently listed as a bird of Panama, although it does occur fairly widely in the mountains of Colombia (Delacour and Amadon 1973:156–157; Hilty and Brown 1986:range map 154). It is conceivable, of course, that its range formerly might have extended to Panama and/or that inhabitants of the isthmus were acquainted with it through their close association with Colombia.

Guans belong to the same family (Cracidae) as curassows and, like them, are slender gallinaceous birds (Delacour and Amadon 1973:chap. 2). Like curassows, they are basically darkish, brown-black birds characterized by brightly colored ornaments, including wattles, dewlaps, horns, or areas of bare skin on face or throat (Delacour and Amadon 1973:Fig. 10, chap. 5; Hilty and Brown 1986:Plate 6). The wattled guan in particular is a large (twenty-eight inches) bird with a small head lacking a crest and a long slender neck, blackish plumage strongly glossed bronze-green, a small bare yellow throat patch and, most significant for the Coclé depictions, a long (two to two-and-a-half inches), round, dangling, bright yellow wattle (Fig. 53) (Hilty and Brown 1986:126, Plate 6; Delacour and Amadon 1973:156–158, Plate 16).

In overall shape the wattled guan, like other guans, has the small head, thin neck, and fowl-like body shape of the tinamou, plus characteristic "appendages," including a definite tail and the colored throat ornaments. This description fits Figs. 50, 10, and 52 rather well, for the small-headed, thin-necked, fowl-like bird with rounded rump depicted here shows a definite wattle; indeed, the wattle (shown more stylized in Fig. 10) seems the most characteristic feature. This bird is also depicted with a definite tail, although the presence of a tail is indicated only by a lightly emphasized line. A slight crest is also portrayed at the back of the head, which brings to mind either the eastern Panamanian subspecies of "basic tinamou" or the crested or purple guan (*Penelope purpurascens*), widely distributed in Central America and northern South America (including Panama), in which the feathers of the crown of the head form a short bushy crest (Delacour and Amadon 1973:136–140; Ridgely and Gwynne 1989:114; Wetmore 1965:298–302). It is also very interesting to note that specimens of crested guan have been found to have reddish clay in their crops, for a clay-eating bird might well be associated with ceramics in a symbolic sense (Delacour and Amadon 1973:140). Wetmore (1965:302) mentions that crested guans give a strangely resonant call, especially toward sunset or as a storm approaches, which also could relate them, like tinamous, to the symbolic potencies of dusk and/or of rain.

The birds in Fig. 50 (in three of the four quadrants) also show a small but distinctive "spiky" marking on the forehead which is slightly more elaborated in Fig. 51 (top l. and bottom r. quadrants), where the wattle is depicted more stylistically (bottom r. quadrant), but the lower bill is brightly colored and wattle-like in shape. The spiky forehead marking strongly suggests the very distinctive bright scarlet and nearly cylindrical casque or horn that protrudes upright from the head of the horned guan (*Oreophasis derbianus*) (Delacour and Amadon 1973:33). Although today the range of this guan is restricted to mountains of Chiapas and Guatemala, Delacour and Amadon note that its range was once more extensive (1973:173). Here, as in the other "guan" portrayals, the major, colorized emphasis is accorded to the identifying wattle and to the rounded tinamou-like shape of the bird's body with the presence of a cracid tail only lightly acknowledged.

Considered overall, this second category of birds emphasizes the basic body form of the tinamou, but in place of the egg depicted with the tinamou figure per se, the guan-like birds add various other bodily appendages—dangling wattle, horn or casque, even possibly a dewlap (perhaps implied in the enlarged lower bill of Fig. 51). It is most interesting, and perhaps not accidental, that in nature both the tinamou egg and the particular ornamental guan appendages chosen for depiction by Coclé artisans are very brightly colored units and that they all appear to "erupt" or emerge from the body of the bird. (In Fig. 47 the tinamou egg is not yet fully laid but is depicted as still emergent, appearing as a fixed protuberance of the bird's body.) The capacity to produce such colorful eruptions may be the physical characteristic symbolically linking all these birds, perhaps marking them all as tinamou-derived producers of fundamental, tinamou-originated color energies.

4 MAMMALS

Judging from a range of design features, numerous types of mammals are represented in the Coclé polychrome ceramics, including the deer (see Figs. 83 and 90; Lothrop 1976:98 middle r., 104 top l., 72 top l., 7 bottom l.); the anteater (Figs. 19 and 36); possibly the tapir (Fig. 20); perhaps the peccary or similar type of animal (agouti, capybara) (Lothrop 1976:58 middle l., 47 middle r.); the monkey or possibly a mythical tailed sloth (Fig. 22); the coati or ring-tailed cat (Fig. 76); the bat (Lothrop 1976:40 bottom r.); and a curly-tailed feline with well-padded clawed paws (Lothrop 1976:108 r., 95 top l.; Cooke 1993).

One of the most commonly depicted mammalian motifs parallels the postulated fundamental-creature-with-appendages theme that has been suggested for serpent-related and tinamou-related designs. For the serpent, the long sinuous body form is basic; for the tinamou, the round-rumped, small-headed bird form is basic. In this third, mammalian mode of expression the basic design motif reveals a frontal view of a standing creature with round mid-section that sometimes contains a central circle and/or other mark. This creature has four long limbs, two serving as support feet or rear paws and two upraised as hands or paws. The variation in appendages attached to this four-limbed but upright creature with a round abdomen is expressed by the presence or absence of a tail, by mode of depiction of the tail, and by mode of depiction of the head.

For reasons that will shortly become clearer, I suggest that the basic mammalian form (if such it is) may refer to the spectacled bear and the many anthropomorphic-cum-symbolic qualities associated with the bear. In general, however, these designs appear more enigmatic than the

FIG. 54. *Quadripartite design featuring two curassows (upper left and lower right quadrants) and two four-limbed creatures with upright stance and bird-like heads. From Lothrop (1976:90).*

FIG. 55. *Frontal view of bird with spread tail and spread wings possibly referencing the eagle. From Lothrop (1976:46).*

other motifs discussed so far, and the interpretation is accordingly more tentative.

Judging by the nature of added appendages, the figures portrayed with round or circled mid-section and upright stance divide broadly into two categories. The first correlates with birds, perhaps particularly the curassow or the eagle; the second correlates with more clearly recognizable mammalian creatures.

The bird category is characterized by a few depictions of creatures with heads turned sideways and indications of head crests and long bills. These portrayals generally occur in overall design clusters (see chapter 7) also featuring the curassow (Fig. 54) or perhaps a guan (Fig. 34). Sometimes (as in these figures) there is no tail (Lothrop 1976:29 r. second from bottom), but on other such bird-like depictions (Lothrop 1976:74 bottom l., 67 bottom) a definite tail is obvious. On all these figures the four limbs are clawed. Though bird motifs are present, the overall mode of depiction is distinctly different from bird portrayals seen before. The association of avian characteristics with rounded mid-section and four limbs as well as the general stance must have conveyed distinctive symbolism, perhaps deliberately associating the galliform birds with mammalian, possibly anthropomorphic, qualities. This association is particularly clear on embossed gold chest plaques from Sitio Conte that portray the same figure: bipedal stance, circular navel, full and banded tail dependent from a belt, and long beaked head, facing sideways, with head crest (see Hearne and Sharer 1992:78–80).

Fig. 55, on the other hand, may point in a different direction. It

appears to portray a frontal view of a tailed bird with two legs and rounded mid-section, the latter surrounded with multiple depictions (judging from the bands) of the curassow or possibly the eagle tail. The upright stance may depict a bird with spread wings, possibly relating this figure to the eagle, which in gold work is shown in an upright stance with spread wings. Although Fig. 55 seems strongly avian, some depictions of a full-frontal creature seem to lead into more mammalian-like depictions. For example, on Fig. 56 the head crest and tail may be somewhat bird-like, but there is a snout rather than a bill (on Lothrop 1976:67 bottom, the head has a beak but the head crest spikes strongly suggest Fig. 56). In all of these depictions the head is turned sideways, which may refer basically to a bird theme.

The other category of "mammalian" figures, in contrast, is characterized by heads facing fully front. Some of these creatures, however, are paired with curassows in overall plate designs. Fig. 57, for example, shows a pair of curassows alternating with a very different type of creature shown with either a thin tail or a Y-element portrayal of mammalian sexuality/fertility and a broad and seemingly flat-faced head with small curved ears. Variants on this theme include a round-headed full-faced creature with no tail paired with a larger-headed creature with a definite tail but lacking elbows and knees (Fig. 58; compare larger-headed creature with Fig. 68, which is more insect-like); a round-headed full-faced creature with or without small round ears and with or without a small tail or perhaps pendulant penis (Figs. 59, 60, and 96; see also Lothrop 1976:102 bottom l.); and a more triangular-headed creature

FIG. 56. *Four-footed and tailed creature in upright stance suggesting mammalian characteristics. From Lothrop (1976:87).*

FIG. 57. *Two curassows alternating with two mammalian creatures characterized by upright stance, round abdomen, and large head possibly referencing the spectacled bear. From Lothrop (1976:15).*

FIG. 58. *Variations on the basic theme of four-legged creatures with upright stance and rounded abdomen. Note that creatures depicted in upper left and lower right quadrant may lack elbows and knees. From Lothrop (1976:13).*

FIG. 59. *Variation on the basic theme of four-limbed creature with upright stance and rounded abdomen. Note small mammalian ears on the round heads. From Lothrop (1976:14).*

FIG. 60. *Further variations on basic theme of four-footed creature with upright stance and distinctive abdomen. From Lothrop (1976:14).*

FIG. 61. *Round-headed, full-faced, frontal stanced creature with distinctive mammalian ears possibly referencing the spectacled bear. From Lothrop (1976:15).*

56

CHAPTER FOUR

(which, if imagined in profile, perhaps suggests the animal would be long-snouted) but with no ears or tail (Fig. 11; see also Lothrop 1976:14 bottom l.). One variant of the round-eared full-face portrayal occurs in more abstract form (Figs. 15, 61, 62, and 63). On Fig. 63 color coding and mode of depiction of upper and lower limb ligatures, as well as the relation of animal legs and ligatures with clawed feet (upper limbs) versus human ligatures with human feet (lower limbs), seems to suggest a humanoid-animal transformation. Figs. 61 and 15 show variations on this portrayal. So do Figs. 64 and 65, which show a curly or round-eared mammalian (humanoid?) female with serpent qualities or with human/animal limb ligatures (Fig. 5).

On Fig. 66 the frontal, full-faced creature with claws, small round ears and round mid-section seems portrayed as a tailed sloth (cf. Fig. 22 and discussion below). On Fig. 67 a similar small-eared front-facing round-tummied creature corresponds to the tail-end of the serpent (or vice-versa). Some variations on the "mammalian" theme seem to be rather insect-like, especially when the tripartite divisions of head, mid-section, and tail are accorded equal graphic weight (Fig. 68; see also Lothrop 1976:24 top r., 24 bottom l. where the mid-section has been elongated to be more bar-like).

Within the context of mammalian-like features, the "limb-and-paw" or "severed-limb" kenning must be considered further, too. Several of the Coclé ceramics depict a curved limb, sometimes ligatured, with paw/foot/claw attached appearing either as a kenning in more complex designs or by itself. One design (Fig. 69) simply shows a paw or foot as a motif—apparently a kenning for an animal—placed in pairs and color

FIG. 62. *Variation on mammalian form shown in Fig. 61. From Lothrop (1976:16).*

FIG. 63. *Basic four-limbed, small-eared mammalian form suggesting, by color coding and mode of depiction of ligatures and feet, human-animal transformation. The human is clearly female, and the animal may be the spectacled bear. From Lothrop (1976:16).*

FIG. 64. *Round-eared female form, possibly referencing both human and bear or bear alone with serpent kennings on limbs. From Lothrop (1976:25).*

FIG. 65. *Variation on the small-eared, four-limbed, upright stanced mammalian form indicating female gender and serpent bar-line kennings and possibly referencing the spectacled bear. From Lothrop (1976:25).*

FIG. 66. *Basic mammalian form as monkey. From Lothrop (1976:17).*

FIG. 67. *Basic mammalian form as tail-end of double-headed serpent motif. From Lothrop (1976:42).*

FIG. 68. *Insect-like variation on basic "mammalian" theme. From Lothrop (1976:24).*

differentiated, in now-familiar fashion, within the ovals of a serpent oval-rectangle pattern; another design (Fig. 70) depicts color-contrasted paws/feet by themselves.

These depictions have more than a generalized mammalian feel about them, for they show a full-footed, plantigrade print made by an animal that stands on the entire sole of the foot with the heel touching the ground. The narrower heel and broader front of the foot is also distinctive. Several zoological possibilities are suggested: the prints may represent human feet; they may represent bear paws; they may be coati paw prints.[1] Let us start with the bear, an animal with especially good credentials as prototype for a mythological and symbolic persona.

If the ceramic designs relate to the bear, they would refer zoologically to the spectacled or Andean bear (*Tremarctos ornatus*), a rarely seen and little-known bear formerly abundant in the Andes[2] that today inhabits territory from six hundred to thirteen thousand feet, most commonly the cooler forests and clearings and lower savannahs of portions of the Andean mountains, including western Venezuela and Colombia and "possibly southern Panama," where unconfirmed sightings have been reported (Van Gelder 1990:733; Walker 1975a:1171; Weinhardt 1993:134). It is certainly conceivable that a thousand years ago the range of the spectacled bear might have included the cordilleras of the isthmus of Panama.

When fully grown the spectacled bear, the only bear native to South America, is about five to six feet in head and body length and stands twenty-eight to thirty-two inches at the shoulder. Like all bears, its ears are small, rounded, and erect, and it has a short stubby (two- to three-inch) tail. The spectacled bear can also be rather striking in appearance

FIG. 69. *A band of plantigrade foot prints with narrower heels and broader fronts, suggesting bear prints, contained within the ovals of boa oval—concave-ended rectangle pattern. Central foot print may be positioned within a boa circle. From Lothrop (1976:49).*

FIG. 70. *Bear-like plantigrade foot prints or feet surrounding possible boa cross-section or boa circle. From Lothrop (1976:29).*

(Fig. 71). Generally speaking, its blackish-brown coat is often marked "with a whitish or yellowish coloration on the muzzle that extends upward to encircle each eye, like comic spectacles, and downward over the throat to the chest, where it forms an irregularly defined ring" (Van Gelder 1990:733; Shepard and Sanders 1985:49–51; Koopman 1991:399; see illustration in Walker 1975a:1171). The eye rings also delineate the snout, making it appear narrower between the eyes and broader across the nose. However, these markings, though characteristic, are extremely variable among individuals and do not appear in a uniform manner on all specimens. The paw print made by the spectacled bear, like all bears, appears very human-like, displaying five digits (actually long non-retractile claws) and with the entire sole touching the ground (Van Rosen 1990:301).

Returning to the Coclé design motifs, I propose that the zoological prototype for the four-footed creature portrayed in upright frontal fashion with a round circle or other marking on its mid-section, with (sometimes) small ears and round eyes, and (in some cases) an elongated nose (Figs. 5 and 57–60) may be the spectacled bear, and that depiction of any four-footed, frontal-stanced upright creature with a marking on a trunk or mid-section may be referencing the bear as basic to the depiction in some manner (Figs. 63–65).

It seems quite plausible that the bear could be one of the fundamental, mythically primordial creatures, along with the Great Snake, the tinamou, and perhaps the sloth (see below), that might have been associated by ancient Panamanians with cosmic creation or beginnings.

FIG. 71. *Spectacled bears* (Tremarctos ornatus). *Facial markings are highly individualistic. Adult bear shown here has only one eye partially ringed but cub shows partial spectacles around both eyes. Photos by Jessie Cohen. By permission of the National Zoological Park, Smithsonian Institution, Washington, D.C.*

FIG. 72. *Standing bear. From Harter (1979:40, Fig. 174).*

This argument rests basically on the very widespread and probably extremely ancient attribution of a wide range of exceptional supernatural qualities to the bear (see Shepard and Sanders 1985; Hallowell 1926; Campbell 1959:334–347; Ingold 1987:249, 256–261; Tyler 1975:chap. 8; Tedlock 1984:263–264). These include association with fearlessness and wildness, rebirth, curing, and success in the hunt, and mediation with the spirit world, particularly as a liminal being that moves between the earth's surface and the underworld or conjoins water, land, and sky with its skills as fisher and swimmer, terrestrial walker, and arboreal climber.

Some associations also undoubtedly reflect in part the very human-like appearance and behavior of the bear (Fig. 72): its frequent use of upright stance, its large head with broad skull, heavy forehead, strong cheekbones, and eyes nearly in a frontal plane; its close attendance on its playful and expressive cubs, including nursing in a sitting position and occasional cuffs and spankings; its plantigrade five-toed footprint and agile use of forepaws for digging, handling, and climbing; its tendency, when walking, to create and utilize narrow trails that look like human footpaths; and its very human-like anatomy when skinned (Shepard and Sanders 1985:chap. 1). In light of such anatomical and behavioral characteristics, the bear is frequently understood to be a furry human, and beliefs in bear-human (shaman) transformation, in the bear as human forefather, or that the bear is kin to humans were and are widespread, as are beliefs that the bear is a kind of animal king or Master of the Animals, is associated with wealth (treasure), and that only chiefs are qualified to hunt bear (Shepard and Sanders 1985:chap. 3; Goldman 1975:147–148, 234; Locher 1932:18–19; Ingold 1987:257).

Although I am aware of only one brief reference to a bear in Pana-manian (Kuna) tales—as a "brother" (along with a number of other ani-mal brothers) of the culture-hero, Ibeorkun (Nordenskiöld 1979:281, 283)—the spectacled bear appears in native lore and traditional belief of the northern Andes.[3] Taussig notes that the well-known traveling native herbalists and healers (Inganos) of southwest Colombia include the dessicated paws of the bear (and of the jaguar) among the various charms and products they sell (1980:237). McDowell (1989), also speak-ing of the Ingano and Kamsá peoples of southwest Colombia (ancient residents of the Sibundoy Valley), says that

There are no longer any bears in the Sibundoy Valley, but the elders still remem-ber seeing them there, and what is more, the bear has left behind quite a presence in the lore of the native communities of the valley. In mythic narrative among the Kamsá and Ingano people, the bear figures as a somewhat oafish character, often the blundering victim of tricksters like the rabbit and the squirrel. In another guise, known generally as the "Juan Orso" tale, the bear as an animal-person shows an unwarranted interest in human females. [McDowell 1989:51]

McDowell also mentions a story concerning the bear and the trickster squirrel that is of particular interest because it includes an episode also found in tales regarding good versus evil or nature versus culture from the Kuna Indians of Panama (Helms 1977:74–80). Both stories involve a physically strong (but apparently not very intelligent) character associ-ated with nature—the bear (also portrayed as the *gobernador* of the com-munity) in the Sibundoy version and an iguana (also initially portrayed as a chiefly leader) in the Kuna version—and a tricky and wily (that is, intelligent) protagonist associated with culture. In both tales the strong-but-dull-witted creature (the bear or the iguana) is tricked into crush-ing his own testicles with a rock at the instigation of the trickster, who then further outwits the dullard and transforms him into an edible rep-tile (Kuna version) or organizes an army of ants and wasps to fight off the soldiers he sends (as *el señor gobernador* in the Sibundoy version) (McDowell 1989:55, 51; Helms 1977:77; cf. Goldman 1975:234).

Another Sibundoy tale, an origins myth, portrays the bear in a more flattering light by describing how an ancestral hunter acquires the nec-essary spirit power to become a Master of Animals, "one who is able to transform himself into the jaguar or the bear" (McDowell 1989:119).[4] (We will note below the possibility that Panamanian art encodes the bear as hunter-cum-Master of Animals with the iguana as his game.) Contact-era accounts by Europeans with reference to Venezuela north of the Orinoco note that "some of the most distinguished warriors were clad in puma or bear skins, with the animal's mouth placed over the head" (Kirchhoff 1948:489).

Consider, too, the *boráro* or *kurupíra,* a fearsome creature of the forest widely known among Amazonian tribes and described by Reichel-Dolmatoff for the Desana, which is also highly suggestive of the bear in many respects. As with several of the comments from above, this description also combines at least one major bear and jaguar motif, and Reichel-Dolmatoff queries whether a single basic concept may ultimately be involved.

Basically, however, the essential creature seems very bear-like. As a supernatural being, the *boráro* is described as a tall naked man with a hairy chest, short hair cut horizontally, and a huge penis. Generalizing from descriptions given by various groups, Reichel-Dolmatoff describes the *boráro* as "a monstrous man-like being, covered with shaggy black hair, with huge fangs protruding from his mouth" (1975:182, 182–190). Its eyes are red and glowing, and its large, curved fangs are like those of a jaguar. Its roar is also likened to that of a jaguar. Its ears are large, erect and pointed forward. As a wild spirit the *boráro* also has various physical anomalies, such as feet twisted backward and no knee joints.

The *boráro* spends much time in the forest or on headwaters of streams where it gathers crabs, its favorite food, although it also eats fruits. Sometimes it is encountered sunning itself in a clearing of the forest. This creature kills unwary hunters by urinating a poisonous stream over them or by enfolding them in a crushing embrace, pulverizing flesh and bones (a characteristic that clearly suggests parallels with constrictor serpents, too). The *boráro* is recognized as a "Chief of the Animals" by the Desana, and Reichel-Dolmatoff wonders whether in the past the *boráro* might have been the Master of Animals. He suggests that the negative image and characteristics accorded the *boráro* today may have developed relatively recently (1971:86–88).

If the range of the spectacled bear included the cordilleras of Panama a thousand years ago, or even if the bear were known to Panamanians only from Colombian and western Venezuelan contacts—and the ancient Panamanians undoubtedly had close ties to northern South American peoples—it would be entirely reasonable to expect that the

bear would be considered as a very "special" animal relative to humans and especially to hunters and to others associated with cosmologically "outside" phenomena, such as chiefs and shamans. Special supernatural qualities very likely were attributed to the bear, and it is even conceivable that Panamanian belief systems recognized shaman-bear transformation. In fact, given the virtually universal attribution of special qualities to bears wherever they have been known, it would be strange indeed if such were not the case.

Emboldened by such argument, we may find additional evidence of bear motifs in Panamanian art if we look more closely at a peculiar "animal-limb-with-paw" kenning frequently found on both ceramic plates and effigy forms where the paws often have flat or only lightly clawed digits. Some of the effigy ceramics are in the form of round-eared creatures sometimes with stubby tails (Figs. 73 and 74; see also Lothrop 1976:38 r.) whose facial designs, with round eyes and marked snout or encircled eyes (Lothrop 1976:36 top l.), are very similar to some of the facial portrayals shown before and strongly suggest the face of the spectacled bear.

FIG. 73. *Effigy bowl depicting stubby tailed, round-headed creature, possibly the bear, with distinctive limb-and-paw design containing serpent-related barline kennings. From Lothrop (1976:37).*

FIG. 74. *Round-eared mammalian effigy with limb-and-paw motif possibly referencing the spectacled bear. From Lothrop (1976:38).*

FIG. 75. *Effigy carafe with banded spout possibly referencing a coati or ring-tailed cat, though stubby tail suggests affinities with the bear or the sloth, too. From Lothrop (1976:65).*

FIG. 76. *Monkey-like creature with banded tail suggesting coati. From Lothrop (1976:43).*

As a cautionary note, however, consider Fig. 75, an effigy with more sharply clawed feet and striped tail. This animal may well be a raccoon or a coati (or ring-tailed cat), which has several characteristics pertinent to design features of the motif in question. The coati (*Nasua narica*), which ranges throughout Central America, is a slender, dark brown or reddish, raccoon-like animal about two feet long with a long head, slender, mobile muzzle and a long tail, lightly ringed with bands of light and dark fur, that is frequently carried aloft. The ears are small and rounded, and the eyes are circled by broken white rings. The feet are plantigrade and the five toes on each paw are strongly clawed (Kaufman 1982:580). The muzzle, chin, and throat are whitish, and the fur on the chest and shoulders is also light colored (Hall and Kelson 1959:891–892).

With respect to Coclé designs, in addition to Fig. 75, occasional depictions on flat plates show a similar ring-tailed creature that also seems monkey-like (Fig. 76) and it is conceivable that the monkey, the raccoon, and the coati were considered separate expressions of the same classificatory "type" of creature in Panamanian ethnozoology. Nonetheless, although the coati seems to be present as a design motif, many depictions of the front-facing, round-eyed and round-eared creature whose chest or abdomen has a distinctive marking do not show the distinctive coati tail, which returns us to the very short-tailed spectacled bear.

The distinctive curved-limb-with-paw motif (often with serpent barline markings as well) depicted on effigy jars that may represent the spectacled bear (Figs. 73 and 74) is also frequently found (sometimes with ligatures) as a kenning on plates and open bowls (Figs. 46 [serpent band ovals], 14 [center bar], 77, and 13 [center and side bars]). Some

depictions of the round-eared, flat-faced creature with round eyes, long nose, and ligatured limbs (e.g., Figs. 63, 64, 65, and 5) also show the same kind of curved limb with paw (see also Lothrop 1976:6 bottom l. [center circle]), suggesting that this creature, now presumably modeled on the bear motif, may be the animal the curved-limb kenning depicts.

These figures are also clearly of female gender, and as such they immediately bring to mind the Kuna concept of Muu, the female power who directs the creation of human souls and life including the forming of the foetus in the womb (Nordenskiöld 1979:372–373). Muu may also be related to the mythological first woman, Great Mother, who is granted recognition as the creator of plants, animals, people (ibid.: 374, 385–386, 437–438). Conceivably, too, these figures depict a Panamanian variant on the very widespread myth of the Bear Mother in which a human girl becomes wife to, or is raped by, a bear and produces mixed Bear Sons who are capable of human-animal transformation and become great hunters (Urton 1985:271; Shepard and Sanders 1985:58–61).[5] This tale proclaims that both bears and people are part-human part-animal, that hunting is a sacramental activity between hunters and animals, and that the bear can mediate between cosmological realms (Shepard and Sanders 1985:59–60).

Possibly Fig. 63 (see also Lothrop 1976:6 bottom l.) indicates, by color coding and the treatment of limb ligatures, just such a theme of human-bear transformation. On this figure the "inner" body and lower limbs and feet of the creature appear to be human, while the "outer" covering of the torso, the upper limbs and claws, and the upper half of the face appear to be different, perhaps animal. This depiction could

FIG. 77. *Underside of plate showing boa oval—rectangle motif with ligatured-limb-with-paw kenning, possibly referencing the bear, in the ovals. Four-quartered center design within boa circle(?) may depict cacao seeds. From Lothrop (1976:89).*

FIG. 78. *Large-headed upright-stanced being, possibly referencing the spectacled bear. From Lothrop (1976:42).*

FIG. 79. *Design from embossed gold breastplate depicting small-eared, large-headed, four-limbed, plantigrade-footed being in upright stance and frontal pose and with distinctive chest marking with iguanas hanging from the waist. Personage may represent the spectacled bear as zoological prototype for a hero-hunter or Master of Animals. After Lothrop (1964:143). By permission of The University Museum, University of Pennsylvania.*

relate to a transformation mytheme or conceivably depicts a human figure wearing a bear skin and bear headdress, again presumably with intent to convey a transformation message. (See above regarding bear headdress worn by warriors in Venezuela.) It is noteworthy, too, that female identification is also found in conjunction with herbivores, as contrasted to male principles associated with predator animals, among Colombian tribes (Labbé 1986:124).

The very distinctive face on Fig. 63 appears by itself in some examples (e.g., Figs. 61 and 15), suggesting that the zoological prototype for these curious faces with small round ears, round eyes, and definite nose or snout is, again, the bear cast in a mythic role and perhaps portraying a Master of the Animals or a version of the Bear Mother or a Great Mother, which is to say, portraying a theme relating to proper human-animal relations or to cultural origins of some sort. The same creature seems to be portrayed full-figured in Figs. 64, 65, and 5, which again depict female figures conveying possible themes of human-animal transformation (Fig. 5) and/or serpent association (note the bar-line motifs on Figs. 64 and 65).[6]

One additional characteristic of the spectacled bear may be expressed in Fig. 78 in the broad head of the body outline within which details of the creature are depicted. The skull of the spectacled bear is described as unusually wide and massive due to the heavy jaw muscles needed by this herbivore for crushing branches and stalks and fruits of palms and other plant material (Shepard and Sanders 1985:50, 53; Walker 1975a:1171; Allen 1942:399). The broad-headed outline on Fig. 78 is common in depictions of front-facing, often elaborately head-crested creatures, shown both in ceramic art and on embossed gold breastplates also from Sitio Conte (Figs. 79 and 80) (Hearne and Sharer 1992:71–72; Helms 1977:94–95).[7] The figures shown on each of the gold pieces depict a four-footed creature in full-frontal pose with two animals, identified elsewhere as iguanas, hanging from his belt (Helms 1977:92–96). These central figures have been described (ibid.) as priest-chiefs or culture-hero deities or hero-hunters or Masters of the Animals carrying game attached (belted) to their waists, as a hunter would do. On the basis of the broad and massive appearance of the head of the central figure, I now offer the additional suggestion that these depictions on both ceramics and gold pieces are based on the spectacled bear as zoological prototype for the hero-hunter or Master of Animals.[8]

If the facial expression of the round-headed, front-facing creatures depicted on flat plates is emphasized alone (separating the matter of plantigrade feet and the limb-with-paw kenning from consideration), another possible zoological prototype should be considered. At least some of these depictions strongly resemble the round head and flat-faced appearance of the tree sloth (*Bradypus* [three-toed] or *Choloepus*

FIG. 80. *Design from embossed gold breastplate with characteristics as described in Fig. 79 (but lacking distinctive chest marking). Note lower limb ligatures. Personage may represent the spectacled bear as zoological prototype for a hero-hunter or Master of Animals. After Easby and Scott (1970: Fig. 238). By permission of The University Museum, University of Pennsylvania.*

FIG. 81. *Squirrel monkey. From Harter (1979:4, Fig. 17).*

[two-toed]) (Lévi-Strauss 1969:355, Fig. 57). This parallel is enhanced in depictions where the paws are shown as strongly clawed and when the flat face with its front-facing eyes has an open or "smiling" mouth (e.g., Fig. 22 and the larger figures in Fig. 58), although, since sloth ears are very inconspicuous (Walker 1975b:488–491), the "sloth hypothesis" weakens when ears are distinctly shown. The presence of a tail on some ceramic depictions could complicate such an identification, too, since the tree sloth's tail is very short or rudimentary.

However, it is interesting to encounter a myth from South America (Mato Grosso) which describes the sloth both as a primordial creature and as once *having had* a tail, which was lost in an interesting manner with by-now familiar consequences. Briefly, the primordial tailed sloth, who was the ancestor of the ancestral birds, refused to share with the birds some ripe fruit that he was eating. Angry at this stinginess, the birds ripped out the sloth's tail, and the blood that flowed from the wound then colored various birds (Pressman 1991:84). Elsewhere, sloths are regarded as the "chiefs" of all the various species of monkeys (Hugh-Jones 1979:193). Since, in general, sloths are accorded important mythological symbolism in tropical America, being associated with primordial conditions, human ancestors, and cultural origins in a number of contexts (Lévi-Strauss 1988:chap. 6, chap. 7, chap. 8), some reference to sloths in Coclé art would not be surprising.

Alternatively, if depiction of a tail *is* taken as part of the essential "key" defining the zoological prototype for this type of figure, then the monkey comes to mind as a possible model. The Central American spider monkey (*Ateles geoffroyi*), for example, is well known for its versatile prehensile tail as well as for long, thin limbs and a large "pot belly" that would admirably fit the characteristic round abdomen and four long limbs of the round-headed figures, even though tails, when depicted, are often only minimally emphasized (smaller figures on Fig. 58 and Figs. 59, 60). In addition, *Ateles geoffroyi panamensis,* the isthmian variant, is characterized by a "mask" of pale, unpigmented skin around eyes and muzzle that in appearance is suggestive of the facial markings of the spectacled bear (Emmons 1990:132–133, Plate 14). However, the squirrel monkey (*Saimiri oerstedii*), could be a possibility, too, not only because of the presence of a tail but again because of distinctive facial markings "[The monkey's] masklike white face contrasts sharply with its black muzzle and black cap of fur and its golden or bronze-colored long limbs and tail often seem to glow in the sun" (Boinski 1992:44, 45). The "masklike white face" presents a distinctly spectacled appearance, with rings of white fur circling the eyes (Fig. 81).[9]

Finally, the creatures depicted on Figs. 58, 59, and 60, as on other drawings of the round-faced and round-tummied creature, also seem to sport several stylized chin whiskers, perhaps indicative of (outlining?) beards. The distinctive beard of the howler monkey comes to mind, although the mode of design portrayal does not appear obviously related. Considered overall, if monkeys are zoological prototypes for the round-headed, round-abdomened and long-limbed creatures (although the absence or only casual depiction of tails is very bothersome here), the depictions may combine distinctive characteristics of several species of monkeys and thus relate to them generically.[10]

All in all, identification of a "basic mammal" in Coclé polychrome ceramic depictions remains problematical, with several possible contenders for that role. Taking both design motifs and "myth-value" into account, I am inclined to favor the bear as the zoological prototype for a "primordial mammal" with the sloth as a variation on the "bear" theme. Monkeys, raccoons and coatis, in turn, could readily be regarded as appendaged, specifically tailed, expressions of the basic mammal form.

5 THE TREE OF LIFE
AND ITS PRODUCTS

In nature, bears—as well as sloths and monkeys—are also associated with trees, particularly the spectacled bear, which not only is an excellent climber but also constructs feeding platforms in trees to support its weight as it feeds on tree fruits and often sleeps in these "nests" (Weinhardt 1993:134, 135, 139; Walker 1975a:1171; Shepard and Sanders 1985:12, 50). In myth the most important tree is the Tree of Life. It is intriguing, therefore, to find the curved-limb-with-paw (bear?) kenning among a number of design formats that may be associated with Tree-of-Life motifs in Coclé art. In native North America the bear is also associated with tobacco as "protector" of the plant and guardian of its growth. Tobacco has long been widely used as a ritual ingredient to connect the cosmic realms, communicate with spirits, and effect cures (Shepard and Sanders 1985:100; Wilbert 1987; Schele and Miller 1986:145; Robicsek 1978; Miller and Taube 1993:169). Ethnohistoric evidence indicates that tobacco was so used in Panama at the time of European contact (Helms 1979:112–116).

Depictions on Coclé ceramics suggest that a plant product of some sort was used in earlier centuries, presumably as a ritual means of connection and communication with the realms of the supernatural. In the center interior or on the bottom of a number of plates and shallow bowls is a four-quartered pattern placed within a circle (compare the Mesoamerican K'an-cross; Freidel, Schele and Parker 1993:93, 94). In some depictions narrow design bands join the center circle to the border, dividing the entire plate into quarters. On others the plate is divided into quarters by plain bands or by equal positioning of four creatures

FIG. 82. *Four crustaceans surrounding a central circle containing four cacao seeds. The central circle itself may represent the cross-section of a cacao pod and/or the boa oval. The four "panels" with serpent kennings from center circle to rim may represent the sides of a quartered Tree of Life. See text for complete interpretation of this design. From Lothrop (1976:4).*

FIG. 83. *Four creatures (deer?) erupting from cacao pods centered upon a cross-section of a cacao pod containing four cacao seeds. From Lothrop (1976:13).*

around the circle (crustaceans [lobsters or crabs], curassows, deer, combination figures [perhaps] of birds with bears or a mixed bear-curassow-deer design are among the creatures depicted) (Figs. 82, 83, and 25; also Figs. 84 and 77, which are the undersides of plates).

The four-quartered central circle motif itself strongly suggests a depiction of the cross-section of a pod revealing four interior seeds. If we assume that the plant in question would have been valued for ritual use, several types of pod-producing plants might be considered, including the algarroba (*Prosopis juliflora* or *P. alba*), the ceiba (or silkcotton) tree (*Ceiba pentandra*)—one of a number of soft-wooded tropical trees, frequently with hollow trunks, that are associated with the mythological Tree of Life from whose interior flowed the waters of the world—or *Anadenanthera colubrina* whose seeds yield a potent snuff or are ingested in drink (Helms 1977:63–64; Lévi-Strauss 1969:184, 186; Lévi-Strauss 1973:392, 467; Bassie-Sweet 1991:81, 121–124, 151, 171; Furst 1974:84–85; Schultes 1972:24–31).

The pods depicted may also represent cacao, mentioned in Talamancan creation tales and curing lore, where the cacao berry is correlated with human souls (Guevara-Berger 1993:382, 383, 387, 377–378). Cacao is also still used in quantities by the contemporary Kuna Indians of Panama in curing and purification rituals, where it is burned in braziers with red peppers or by itself so that the smoke may drive away evil spirits (Stone 1962:55, 57–58; Stout 1947:36; Sherzer 1983:111, 113; Helms 1979:114). As is well known, cacao has long been widely utilized as a currency, as a ceremonial beverage, for the sweet pulp surrounding the seeds, and as a symbolically important plant in Mesoamerica, native

FIG. 84. *Underside of plate showing four crustaceans surrounding a cross-section of a cacao pod with four seeds. From Lothrop (1976:89).*

Central America including Panama and Costa Rica, and northern South America (e.g., Fowler 1989:159, 162, 108–110; Nordenskiöld 1979:350; González and González 1989:69, 137; Landa 1978:34–35; Stone 1962:44, 65; Stone 1984:68–75; Schultes 1984:32–33; Miller and Taube 1993:Fig. on 135).

Cacao is also a likely candidate for the Coclé design motif because of the shape of its seeds (beans), the manner in which these seeds are layered one on top of the other in neat cells or rows within the pod, and the peculiar growing habit of the pods themselves. *Theobroma cacao,* the common cacao, is a twenty- to twenty-five-foot tree that produces small flowers, and then pods, directly from the leafless trunk and larger (main) branches (Bailey 1917:3330; Janick et al. 1981:22–24). The elliptic-ovoid (football-shaped) pods—red, yellow, purplish, or brown in color—may grow up to a foot in length and are about four inches (or less) in diameter. Internally a pod contains five longitudinal cells, each of which contains a neat stack of five to twelve brown or purple "beans" or seeds embedded in pulp (Bailey 1917:3330).

If a cross-sectional cut were made across a cacao pod, exposing the five cells, each cell section would reveal a flat bean. The beans of *T. cacao* are approximately triangular in shape, with outside edges convexly curved (Janick et al. 1981:612, Figs. 22–24), a shape exactly like those depicted in the Coclé central circle designs (Fig. 85). The packaging of beans within a cross-sectioned pod is also exactly as portrayed in the Coclé designs, except that the designs contain four, rather than five, sections or cells within the cross-sectioned pod (circle). This deviation from nature can readily be understood as a symbolic device, perhaps referencing the four-quartered or four-directional cosmos basic to much tropical American cosmology.

There may be additional depictions of a cacao motif in the Coclé designs. Fig. 83, for example, shows the quadriparte center circle, complete with beans, and four "spokes" (in lieu of panels) radiating outward toward the edge of the plate to become the "tails" of what may be (at least in part) deer. Each of the spokes contains a nested series of concave lines, and each nested series, when considered together with the overall shape of the spokes, could also represent a cell of beans within the cacao pod (see also the body of the bird in Fig. 43). (Several other designs in Lothrop [1976:18 top r., 29 top l.], in their entirety, may depict cacao pod cross-sectional cuts with each of the four bean quarters now depicted as a serpent-related creature or by kennings.) It is intriguing, too, that the colors of cacao pods—red, purple, brown, or yellow—are the same colors (if yellow be equated with white or beige) that predominate in the Coclé designs.

Additional correlations may be suggested between the triangular "cacao bean" depiction and the—also triangular—V-element, which is also sometimes shown in the cluster of four within a central circle (see Fig. 25). Since the V-element has been associated with boa markings in previous discussion, we can now consider whether a thematic relationship may have connected cacao with the Great Serpent motif in some way. Figs. 82 and 77 are interesting in this regard because the proposed central pod with cacao beans seems to be positioned within a possible boa oval (circle).[1] In Fig. 77 the pattern surrounding the central cacao pod very clearly indicates a boa pattern with bear paws in the ovals and the intervening rectangles indicated by Y-element kennings.

One of the thematic connections relating cacao and the serpent concerns the mythical Tree of Life. In myths of tropical America in general this tree (frequently the ceiba), by its roots, trunk, and canopy, conjoins the underworld, the earth's plane, and the sky as an axis mundi. Its leafy canopy contains the creatures of the world, the Great Serpent may nestle in its branches, its base is guarded by giant beings, and when the tree is felled the waters of the world and various life forms gush from its hollow trunk (e.g., Helms 1977:64; Roe 1989:16–17; Lévi-Strauss 1973:102–103, 467; Schele and Freidel 1990:66–67, 70, 72, 418; Miller and Taube 1993:186, 57; Freidel, Schele, and Parker 1993:53, 57, 78–79, 394–396).

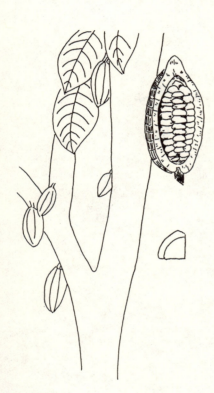

FIG. 85. Theobromo cacao, *the common cacao. Adapted from Bailey (1917:3330, Fig. 3793).*

More specifically, in myths of the Kuna Indians of Panama, a primordial World Tree rises from earth to touch the sky, forming a direct link between earth and sky. The tree is defended by a giant snake, along with a great puma and giant toad (cf. Lévi-Strauss 1973:336). Attempts to fell the tree are foiled by the giant protectors, who must be killed before the disjunction between celestial and terrestrial worlds can occur. After the protectors are killed and the tree falls, fresh and sea waters are released from its trunk and fish, edible plants, and all manner of birds and beasts are created (Nordenskiöld 1979:162–163, 174–179). In myths of the nearby Talamancan peoples of southern Costa Rica, where the tree (the ceiba) falls after it is bent into a circle and is transformed into the water that encircles the earth, the snake is again involved with the World Tree, not in the context of hindering its destruction but of bringing about its original growth (González and González 1989:96–97, 108–109; see also Stone 1962:53–54; Bozzoli de Wille and Cubero 1988:84–86).

Since cacao grows directly from the trunk of a tree, cacao addresses very directly the theme of conjunction and communication between earth and sky contained in the Tree-of-Life motif. The arc of the rainbow serpent relates earth and sky in similar fashion. In addition, just as the mythical serpent produces the distinctiveness of animal and bird life from its bodily fluid (blood) and flesh after it is "felled" (killed) and demolished, so the hollow trunk of the Tree of Life produces life from its waters after it is felled (demolished). It can also be said that for all three entities—the Tree of Life, the Great Serpent, and the cacao pod— the crucial communicative or generative power or characteristic is "contained within" the outward form and is only revealed when the tree, the serpent, or the pod is opened and the inherent or interior essence exposed.[2] This shared quality could have rendered all three appropriate mythical and ritual materials in ancient Panamanian ideological life.[3]

In a previous publication (Helms 1981:4–6), I argued (building on ideas proposed by Heather Lechtman) that indigenous Panamanian art forms, both verbal and plastic, have utilized expository styles which emphasize the revelation of "that which is within," indicating that the real value of something (and someone) is found in qualities located inside the being or thing. The verbal oratory of contemporary Kuna leaders expresses this form when the esoteric archaic language reserved by village chiefs for chants and orations is "translated" by interpreters into the vernacular for listeners, thereby explaining or exposing, for the populace, the meaning "hidden" in the chief's original words (Howe 1974:chap. 3; Sherzer 1974:264–271). The use of reverse appliqué sewing technique in the production of the multicolored panels, called molas, used in Kuna women's blouses expresses this expository form by layering several pieces of cloth and then creating designs by cutting through the top layer to reveal or expose the colors of underlying layers (Helms 1981:4, References). In pre-Columbian Panama the use of herbal baths (*mise-en-couleur*) to produce a shiny gold surface on gold-copper alloy (tumbaga) metal pieces by removing the surface impurities (copper) that "hid" the full golden expression had the same effect of "revealing" the golden quality that was seemingly "hidden" within (Lechtman 1975:10, 1979).

Given these usages, it seems appropriate not only to appreciate the further expression of this theme in conjunction with cacao pods, Great Snakes, and Trees of Life but also to consider whether designs on Coclé ceramics have been constructed in comparable fashion to "reveal that which is within."[4] Several instances of this mode of expression have already been suggested, including the depiction of creatures situated within, or emerging from, the boa oval; the depiction of serpent markings, including bar-line kennings, as constituting part of or contained within the body form of animals; the depiction of a Y-element as viscera inside an animal form, as in the deer (Lothrop 1976:104 top l.) and the tinamou (Fig. 47); the emergence of brilliantly colored eggs from the outwardly drab tinamou; and the suggested cross-sectional representation of the cacao pod that reveals the beans contained inside.

Another use of this motif may be found in overall plate designs, such as Fig. 82. To appreciate this design we must imagine that the overall design motif reveals what would be found "within" if an upright columnar form were slit lengthwise into quarters from the top down and the four quarters spread out, as when an apple is quartered by two ninety-degree cuts across the top. If we were to put the pieces of Fig. 82 back together, that is stand the quarters upright, the serpent kenning panels would become a four-sided (serpent-sided) column with the cacao pod at the base and/or as the interior of the column and the four creatures—apparently lobsters in this example—folded within. Considering this reconstituted structure in mythic or symbolic terms, the columnar structure may be construed as a cacao-producing Tree of Life-cum-serpent with aquatic creatures contained therein or as a Tree of Life-cum-serpent containing aquatic creatures that rests upon a sacrificial cache of cacao beans which, in turn, may be metaphor for sacrifice of a more literally human form, since chocolate may also signify human blood (Guevara-Berger 1993:378; Stone 1962:49). Such an interpretation finds partial support in the Talamancan tale which describes how, when the World Tree fell, marine animals were created from its leaves and from the birds, nests, and eggs that it sheltered (Bozzoli de Wille and Cubero 1988:85; see Miller and Taube 1993:186 regarding very similar portrayals of the World Tree in Mesoamerican art.)

It is also interesting that among the Coclé plate designs depicting a central circle with an animal or cacao seeds contained within, several also include an encircling serpent motif which may conceivably relate to the giant serpent coiled at the base of the Tree of Life in Kuna myth (e.g., Figs. 41 and 77; see also Lothrop 1976:9 bottom r., 42 top). Tangential support for these interpretations may possibly be found in a structurally inverted Sumu (eastern Nicaragua) story about a boy who became a gigantic boa (after eating an improper fish and drinking too much water) and was found by the people on the branches of a very tall ceiba tree (Conzemius 1932:130–131)[5] as well as in the symbolism accorded the shape and construction of the traditional circular Talamancan house in which the base is associated with the serpent (also with the spiral and the paths of the planets), while the center of the circular floor is associated with the center of the world, creation, the cosmic mountain, the World Tree, and sky pillars (González and González 1989:14).

Within the context of cosmologically related communications involving ritual use of an organic substance, such as cacao, some of the mammalian effigy jars mentioned above require further consideration. A number of these jars, as well as simpler rounded jars, called whistling or spouted jars in the literature, feature a slim, hollow protuberance with a narrow opening at the top sometimes in addition to the regular mouth of the jar (e.g., Figs. 33 and 75; Lothrop 1976:32 bottom, 34, 36 bottom, 38, 56–57, 63, 66). The possibility should be considered that these jars, though seeming rather large for the purpose (five to ten inches in height) may have been used as snuffing pots and that they contained substances that were inhaled by means of the slender spouts, now recognizable as nosepieces, which are identical to the spouts of other snuff jars from South and Central America, including Costa Rica, although the overall pot form and size may vary (Fig. 86) (Furst 1974:75, 77; Wassén 1965:25; Wassén 1967:243).

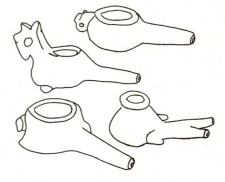

FIG. 86. *Bird-shaped ceramic snuffers from Costa Rica. From Wassén (1965:25, Fig. 2). By permission of Göteborg Etnografiska Museum and Henry Wassén.*

THE TREE OF LIFE

The substance(s) snuffed could have included any number of plant hallucinogens available either locally or by long-distance trade, including *Anadenanthera, Piptadenia, Mimosa, Banisteriopsis* (see Schultes 1972; Furst 1974:86–87). It is very likely that tobacco was among the plants so used, since it was still ritually ingested (by inhaling the smoke of very large cigars) in Panama at the time of European contact (Helms 1979:112) and has a very wide and very crucial ritual use throughout native America in general, including ingestion as snuff (Schultes 1972:53–54; Wilbert 1972:55–57; Wilbert 1987). Toasted tobacco powder is also sometimes used in combination with other vegetal hallucinogens (Wilbert 1972:56; Wilbert 1987:50; Wassén 1965:15, 25; Wassén 1967:271–272). Cacao could have been used as part of a snuff mixture, too; there is ethnographic evidence from Colombia of ash prepared from the bark of the wild cacao tree being mixed with powdered Virola resin to provide an alkaline substance that enhances the narcotic effect of the hallucinogen (Wassén 1965:56, 82–83; Reichel-Dolmatoff 1975:20–21).[6]

The use of hallucinogenic materials in the ritual life of ancient Panamanian peoples may also be indicated by a rather enigmatic cylindrical form (Lothrop 1976:85 top l.), which could conceivably be the stem or base of a mushroom-shaped vessel which has lost its cap. (Stone shows several very similar pieces intact from Costa Rica [1977:Fig. 30, Fig. 31].) Furst (1974:58–64) has discussed the ritual use of mushrooms in ancient Mesoamerica and South America, including Colombia (see also Schultes and Bright 1981), and there is no particular reason to think that they were not so used in Panama. In fact, it is conceivable that the high-based and flat-topped pedestal plates (Fig. 87) in the Coclé ceramic tradition could be stylistically related to mushrooms.

Considered overall, a considerable corpus of material suggested by Coclé design styles and ceramic shapes addresses the possibility of the ritual use of various hallucinogenic plants in ancient Panamanian ceremonies. Conceivably, too, some of the motifs depicted on these wares were derived from hallucinatory experiences, as Reichel-Dolmatoff has suggested for the Tukano (1972:104–113; Reichel-Dolmatoff 1978b; Helms 1977:114–115) and Eger (1978:40, 41, 47, 52) for the Huichol. Possibly the overall zigzag patterns painted on some plates relate to hallucinogenic effects (Lothrop 1976:3 top, 5 lower l., 39 center, 94 lower r.). In addition, some Tukano wall paintings of hallucinatory patterns are

almost identical to boa markings and to the Coclé boa design (Reichel-Dolmatoff 1975:Fig. 58, Fig. 64). Certainly the visions seen by Tukano men when tobacco is smoked and *yajé* (*yagê*) (*Banisteriopsis*) is taken are suggestive of some of the design motifs on the Coclé pieces. Like so many of the Coclé ceramic depictions, "they begin with the snake ..." (Reichel-Dolmatoff 1975:150–151). Taussig elaborates: "hundreds of snakes appear ... and then they form into one enormous boa, which is the owner of *yagé*. He may wind himself around you. Death is imminent. Then the boa straightens out and carries you up into the heavens where the *yagé* people come to teach you about the heavens and introduce you to the spirits who live there. You have left your body. You are dead" (Taussig 1987:321–322).[7]

FIG. 87. *Pedestal plate. This ceramic form may be stylistically related to mushrooms. From Lothrop (1976:106).*

6   BODY PARTS
AND PROCESSES

The depictions of various creatures on the Coclé polychrome designs encode cosmological and sociological themes not only by the choice of specific zoological life forms but also by mode of depiction of particular body parts. Some of these characteristics have been discussed above as aids in identifying the possible zoological prototypes for the various ideological fauna. However, several seem to go beyond species-specific identifications per se to relate to broader themes. Among these are the severed human leg, the open and toothed mouth, and the extended tongue. All of these body parts are commonly encountered in myths, where they are used to convey an immensely wide range of cosmological and sociological themes. It is not possible to become very specific when relating particular body-part depictions in Coclé art with the diverse themes suggested by myths, but some suggestive relationships seem to appear and, at the very least, the use of such motifs in the Coclé art should be recognized.

Let us begin with the severed-leg motif, which appears most often in association with curassow depictions. The severed human leg (with ligatures) appears most obvious in Fig. 4, where it parallels the tail of the bird's serpentine body form, replacing the barred tail seen in other curassow depictions (Fig. 43). It may also form the head crest of Fig. 44 where color coding relates it to the bird's legs. In Fig. 25 the severed limb appears as head crest with strong parallel to the bird's "tail."

As was noted in chapter 3, the severed-leg motif is very familiar to students of Mesoamerican ideology and symbolism. The all-encompassing Mexican god Tezcatlipoca-Huitzilopochtli in his human guise was depicted as lame, either club-footed or bereft of one foot, or in some depictions, of one leg. "His missing foot was the symbol of things that coil around themselves in a spiral motion" like certain constellations, whirlwinds and hurricanes, tornadoes and waterspouts that seem to take the form of a giant leg and foot coming down from the sky and walking across the landscape (Hunt 1977:242, 241, 245; Robicsek 1978:104). In the case of the Mayan God K (K'awil or GII) (who is also depicted in conjunction with the double-headed serpent theme) either the leg in question is transformed into a serpent (Schele and Freidel 1990:414; Freidel, Schele, and Parker 1993:193–196) or one foot is replaced by a serpent head (Schele and Miller 1986:49; Robicsek 1978:68, 71, 74; Miller and Taube 1993:164–165, 110).[1]

In South American myth, the severed leg may spring to life as the tinamou as Mother of Birds (Lévi-Strauss 1964:110) or be associated with the constellation Orion (Lévi-Strauss 1968:106). A myth was recounted above concerning a child who was rising to the sky in a lavishly decorated pot when his leg was severed, the blood from the wound producing multicolored plumage in birds.[2] In these contexts the associations attributed to the severed leg parallel those accorded the rainbow serpent in its role as creator of animals' coloration and in its identity as Master (creator) of painted ceramics.[3] Through association with long bones the severed-leg theme also relates to human ancestors, who are often tangibly correlated with the long bones of the leg (Hugh-Jones 1979:144–145; see chap. 3, note 3).[4] Ancestors, of course, are also associated with Great Snakes, such as the anaconda.

The severed limb is also part of a much larger genre of native American mythemes involving severed or battered body parts of mythical personages not only as source of identifying coloration or markings on birds and animals, as we have seen, but also as life-giving sources of plants, bees and honey, fish, certain constellations (Orion and the Pleiades) and other heavenly bodies, and the rainbow (Labbé 1986:24; Lévi-Strauss 1968:38, 46–47, 51, 95–98, 106–107; Lévi-Strauss 1969:243–246). One example of this genre of myth is found in a version of Talamancan (Costa Rica) creation tales in which a young girl or boy was trampled underfoot by dancers; from the mangled flesh and blood (which, in the case of the girl, also symbolized the first act of menstruation) came the fertile earth that covered the heretofore bare rock, followed by plants, animals, and people (González and González 1989:66–67, 134–137; cf. Reichel-Dolmatoff 1978b:4, 5; in other versions of the Talamancan tale it is a baby jaguar or little child from the under-world who is crushed; see Stone 1962:54–55). It is probable that both this form of bodily destruction and the felling of the World Tree men-tioned above with reference to Kuna myth—both forms of "severing" that open the way for the creation of various categories of animals and plants—are related to the severed-limb theme that associates the cre-ation or identification of life forms with the blood of a child's torn limb or other mangled bodily remains.

It is interesting, too, that some of these Talamancan creation myths appear to be structural inversions of South American tales. In the Tala-mancan tales of children trampled by dancers, a child is a) trampled below, b) into the earth, c) by dancers, creating mangled flesh and blood that produces fertile earth and life forms. In the South American tale of the child who lost his leg while rising to the sky, a child a) rises above, b) to heaven, c) in a decorated earthenware pot, creating a mangled limb that produces faunal distinctiveness. The parallel between dancing and decorated (painted?) ceramics seems to relate to the general theme of artistry as creation. This, in turn relates to the mythical crafting (cre-ation) of a colorful living and ordered world out of the primordial, uncrafted formlessness of death and destruction, such as a dead snake, a torn limb, a trampled child, or a felled World Tree (cf. Hugh-Jones 1979:249–250).

As was noted above, the Coclé severed leg is depicted in association with the curassow, which raises again the possibility that in zoological terms the bird in question might, in fact, be an eagle since in Mesoamerican association of the severed-leg theme with Tezcatlipoca the eagle represents the solar manifestation of the deity. However, Tez-catlipoca's "commonest theophanic form" was the turkey (Nicholson qtd. in Hunt 1977:60), which corresponds well with the proposed association of the severed leg with gallinaceous cracids in Coclé art.

The severing of body parts can also be understood as one way of "opening" a body form. Openness can be depicted in other ways, too. One of the more obvious Coclé motifs is the open mouth with exposed teeth and sometimes protruding tongue which is virtually ubiquitous in portrayals of many mammals (including deer and "bear," among others), serpents, and saurians ("legged serpents") which are sometimes described as "laughing." Various forms and expressions of openness (including laughter) and closure, particularly openness or closure of bodily apertures, are frequent native American (indeed universal) mythemes (e.g., Lévi-Strauss 1969:125–126; Lévi-Strauss 1988: chap. 6, chap. 12; cf. Douglas 1975:83–89).

Openness in the form of laughter, especially uncontrollable or forbidden laughter, often has serious, even disastrous consequences in myths. It is related to nature, wildness, excess, incontinence, or general lack of control and is contrasted with the emotional constraint and self-control associated with culture and social order (e.g., Lévi-Strauss 1969:120–124, 134; Hugh-Jones 1979:195–203). However, good things can be derived from laughter, too, such as the origin of cooking fire, which in a Tucuna tale came from flames issuing from the open, laughing mouth of a swallow, or the openness in expression that comes with creation of articulate speech (language) (Lévi-Strauss 1969:132). In some myths the creation of openings in the body by unplugging an orifice—a closed mouth or a blocked anus, for example—produces the flow of blood that colors birds (Pressman 1991:85, 86).[5]

Considering serpents in particular, in Mesoamerican art the open mouth of the snake is featured in depictions of many deities (Miller and Taube 1993:149). In Mayan iconography the serpent's open jaws formed the portal to the otherworld of the dead (Freidel, Schele, and Parker 1993:370), and in Central Mexican art open-mouthed serpents represented caves, the entrance to the underworld and the realm of the dead (Miller and Taube 1993:56; Bassie-Sweet 1991:chap. 4). Conceivably the open mouths of Coclé serpents carried a comparable connotation of entrance to or communication with another realm.

If so, the sharply toothed open mouths of the Coclé Great Serpent and derivative saurian forms may also relate to a very distinctive characteristic of great snake behavior. Referring again to Lévi-Straussian themes, Roe comments upon the manner in which the giant serpent of the Amazon devours its prey. With its "huge, toothy" mouth the anaconda doesn't only eat its prey raw but "gobble[s] it up in a most 'unseemly,' gluttonous, or 'excessively oral' manner," eating without chewing "as proper humans, or even Jaguars do." Instead it unhinges its mandible and swallows its victims whole (Roe 1989:10). This practice, together with the propensity of the great serpents, when disturbed, to regurgitate their prey, also probably contributes to the idea that creatures enter into, pass through, and emerge in their entirety from the body of the great snake (Hugh-Jones 1979:217; Drummond 1981:644–645). This concept is also indicated by depictions on Coclé ceramics of animals deriving from boa ovals and is seen in Mayan iconography when deities, like God K (K'awil) and the Maize god, emerge from the otherworld via the mouth of the Great Snake (Vision Serpent) (Freidel, Schele, and Parker 1993:196).[6]

In the vast majority of Coclé designs featuring open-mouthed creatures, however, either nothing emerges or only a tongue protrudes (Figs. 21, 23, 35, and 90; see also Lothrop 1976:12, 13 l., 40 lower r., 78 lower l., 100 center l., 104 top l.). Occasionally, however, the tip of the protruded tongue takes the form of a (serpent?) head (Lothrop 1976:8 lower l.), possibly expressed as a Y-form kenning (Fig. 35). In Coclé art, therefore, there is little to evidence oral regurgitation (as distinct from emergence of life forms from boa ovals). There is no overt evidence of ingestion, either. However, it is possible that the portrayal of creatures with open mouths and, sometimes, extended tongues relates to eating. In this context it should be noted that in linguistic and symbolic terms eating is very often related to copulation. Thus the "open-mouth" motif in Coclé art may refer to codes of proprieties or improprieties in human sexual and/or affinal relations.[7]

"Openness" of bodily orifices may also refer to the cleansing of the interior of the body as in sneezing (Hugh-Jones 1979:281, note 23), vomiting or anal discharges. Cleansing, in turn, may relate to the use of hallucinogenic drugs, since ingestion of such materials can result in vomiting, diarrhoea, or excessive mucous discharges from the nose. In this context "openness," combined with the trance experience itself, becomes related to communication with supernatural realms (Hugh-Jones 1979:200), a role accorded to open-mouthed serpents in Mesoamerican iconography (see above and Concluding Remarks) and very likely intended for Coclé serpents (and other open-mouthed creatures), too.

Portrayal of teeth in the open mouth in Coclé art may have additional significance. Teeth are considered by many indigenous peoples of South America to contain whatever unusual powers or mystical energy may be associated with a given animal (Karsten 1926:123–126). Among the Kuna a slightly different interpretation is found. Howe notes (1975:18–20) that teeth or "toothness" identifies importance or strength, particularly in metaphors associated with chiefship in which "large important animals," such as parrots and tapirs and other large mammals, all of which "have teeth," refer to important people or people "with names," such as curers and chiefs.[8] In contrast, common people are compared to "toothless" birds and insects as "unimportant" beings, "people without names."

In Coclé depictions some open-mouth designs (especially of deer and of saurians) also depict a large and protruding tongue (Figs. 35, 23, 83, and 90; see also Lothrop 1976:72 top l., 12). In some cases the broad, fleshy shape of the tongue may identify the creature zoologically as an iguana (Helms 1977:69, 98), but the protruding tongue undoubtedly encodes additional sociological-symbolic messages. In myths from South American the absence or loss of a tongue can refer to improper or ineffective mediation or communication both socially and cosmologically, to disjunction between cosmological realms, or to inability to enforce proper control over improper behaviors (e.g., as a result of unduly loquacious behavior, inability to warn against danger, or greediness and rapaciousness) (Lévi-Strauss 1969:113–120; Lévi-Strauss 1973:228–229; cf. Helms 1977:57, 62). In Central America a Talamancan tale describes how greedy and immoderate behavior caused the caiman to lose its tongue (Stone 1962:66; Helms 1977:68). Presumably exaggerated evidence of possession of a tongue, as in Coclé art, also addresses themes of communication and behavioral controls in some manner.

Among the latter, fertility and sexuality may be involved, especially in depictions of deer, which are metaphorically related to birth and children by the Kuna, and in depictions of the iguana, where the tongue may be associated with the sun's rays, which carry phallic or fertilizing symbolism in tropical American (including Central American) myths (Helms 1977:62–63, 68–71; Helms 1981:57).[9] Such tongues may also relate to speech, either as an attribute of properly conducted social living in general or as an attribute of chiefship when, as in traditional Panamanian society, the duties of chiefship include public oratory and social admonishments (Helms 1977:98). It is fascinating, too, to read the following account of the final initiation of a Mayan shaman in Belize some sixty years ago. Briefly, after retiring to an isolated place for a period of instruction with his teacher, the initiate was "sent to meet" a supernatural being who took the form of a large snake, "very big, not poisonous and having a large shiny eye." When the initiate and the snake met face to face the snake reared up on his tail and put his tongue in the initiate's mouth, thereby communicating the final mysteries of shamanism (Freidel, Schele, and Parker 1993:208–209).

Finally, before leaving the subject of body parts and processes, the "tear-eye" motif, an eye with one corner elongated, is sometimes found on Coclé polychrome designs (Figs. 10 [center], 26, and 88; see also Lothrop 1976:8 top r., 19 top). I could find no completely consistent association with particular animal forms, though the tear-eye seems to appear most often on serpent-related motifs involving chin "whiskers." The tear-eye may, therefore, relate to Sibu, the Talamancan creator-deity, and the giant serpent described in chapter 2. Or, perhaps better said, the serpent face depicted with the combination of tear-eye, whiskers, and open "smiling" mouth may identify a Sibu-related Great Serpent theme or being. Tears per se are a widespread motif in native American symbolism and may be associated with rain and/or with supplications to the sun for pity (see Labbé 1986:155; Thompson 1970:211, 259). In Maya cosmology tears are among the many powerful "special liquids and essences" thought to be blessed substances of the sky (Freidel, Schele, and Parker 1993:51, 411, note 19, 413, note 31). In a Talamancan myth tears create animals (González and González 1989:136–137). Conceivably, too, the tear-eye carried an association with salt water or "bitter" water and connotes contexts or associations with the sea. Considered overall, the suggested association of tears and the tear-eye motif with the giant serpent, the creation of animals, and, possibly, the sea suggests that tears and the tear-eye motif ultimately may relate in a more fundamental sense to the serpent-guarded Tree of Life whose interior waters produced the sea and diverse life-forms.

FIG. 88. *Serpentine creature with the "tear-eye" motif. From Lothrop (1976:26).*

7 WHOLE-PLATE DESIGNS

To appreciate the sophistication of Coclé ceramic designs it is also necessary to go beyond representations of particular motifs to consider the design formats of ceramic pieces in their entirety. Although the symbolism presumably accorded particular motifs may be expected to remain reasonably constant, the positioning of individual motifs within a larger design field may well express wider or more complex processual conditions or event categories. We have seen one example of this in chapter 5 in the discussion of cacao and the Tree of Life motif. In this chapter several additional (although by no means all) whole-plate design styles will be analyzed.

The first such design style to be discussed divides the plate into two equal halves, sometimes with a central bar making the division. In some examples the two halves contain identical or mirror-image depictions, strongly suggesting the general theme of duality (e.g., Figs. 14, 39, 46, 15, 61, and 35). Some of these depictions may also express the theme of "exposing that which is within." These designs seem to represent a single image that was split down the middle (so to speak) and the two halves then opened flat. The "interior" is revealed as the center panel or bar, which may depict various creatures, including some form of serpent motif, possibly in association with a serpent "path" (the length of the bar) such as the Milky Way, or life forms associated with the Tree of Life theme (e.g., crustaceans, as in Lothrop 1976:7 lower l.) relating to a context of cosmological origins (Figs. 14, 46, 15, and 17).

A few of the plates express the imagery of the two halves in contrasting colors (Fig. 89; see also Fig. 93), one half and the central bar being red and the other half blue/black, possibly representing different

FIG. 89. *Hemispheric design format with one half contrasted with the other by color. Note that the entire rim is red, encompassing the blue/black half within the red domain. From Lothrop (1976:21).*

FIG. 90. *Whole-plate design format as expression of the head-end—equals—tail-end or double-headed serpent motif. Here the creatures appear to be at least partially deer. From Lothrop (1976:13).*

FIG. 91(a). *Whole-plate design format conveying double-headed creature motif if the creatures in the lower left and upper right quadrants are considered the two heads (deer and curassow, respectively), while the identical creatures (perhaps bear-related mammals) in the other two quadrants, together with the central panels and cacao seed circle, constitute the single body form conjoining the two heads. From Lothrop (1976:13).*

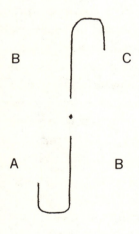

FIG. 91(b). *Schematic diagram of Fig. 91(a).*

conditions or periods of being—perhaps day and night, or the celestial world and the underworld—separated by the earthly plane (the central bar) as recognized by contemporary Talamancan peoples (González and González 1989:88–89). (It is also possible that single-figure designs such as the one Fig. 4 depicts could have referenced a tripartite cosmos in a similar fashion: the head of the bird perhaps representing the celestial realm, the serpent body the terrestrial plane, and the legs the underworld.) Note, too, how in Fig. 89 the red color of one half is also found in the central bar and around the rim of the plate such that the blue/black half is encased within the red domain. This color coding may again express a context of "that which is within." Such modeling also brings to mind the asymmetrical relationship of symbolic inferiority and superiority between social halves—moieties—that yet compose a whole as found, for example, among the Bororo of Brazil (Crocker 1969:54–55).

Very likely the particular colors chosen for such designs conveyed much basic meaning, too. Taking clues from indigenous belief systems of tropical America, we can suggest that red may have correlated with the rising sun and the east, that is, with light and life, while blue/black could have referenced the west and the setting sun, that is, the dark and night (Bassie-Sweet 1991:23). Conceivably, in Fig. 89 the continuation of red around the rim of the blue/black half depicts the nocturnal movement of the sun around the realm of the underworld before rising again in the east. Alternatively, these colors might differentiate the vertical layers of the cosmos: the celestial, the earthly plane, and the underworld (González and González 1989:148–151; Howard 1991:56–57).

A second type of whole-plate design appears as a variation on the head-end–equals–tail-end or double-headed serpent motif. A straightforward example of this style is seen in Fig. 90 in which the two deer compose the double-heads conjoined by a single tail bar. This same motif may be expressed in quartered designs, too, if the overall positioning of the various animals and, sometimes, the use of color are taken as guidelines. Consider, for example, Fig. 91(a) in which the constituent designs can be reduced to basic units (A, B, C)—see Fig. 91(b). This design format may be read as A equals head-/tail-end, and C equals head-/tail-end, while B plus central panel and circle plus B equal the body form conjoining A and C. Alternatively A and C may be seen as head-ends of two separate but identical body forms (each composed of B plus half the central bar) with tail-ends meeting at the

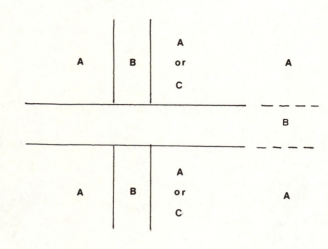

FIG. 92(a). *Multiple double-headed motifs. One set is created by each hemisphere, when the two quadrant designs are conjoined by the panel between them. Another double-headed motif is found when each hemisphere is conjoined by the central panel. From Lothrop (1976:20).*

FIG. 92(b). *Schematic rendering of format of Fig. 92(a).*

circle. Fig. 93 is comparable. The two dark quarters constitute identical head-/tail-ends conjoined by the two other quarters and the central panels, all of which are conjoined by the same color.

This type of whole-plate design may also contain another more abstract "layer" of double-headed serpent motif which, in turn, yields a third type of whole-plate design. Consider Fig. 26, in which the basic design units can be identified, first, with respect to each half (abc or cba) and, second, with respect to the two halves and the central bar as overall design (ABA). The overall design composed of both halves (A and A) plus the central bar (B) becomes a double-headed serpent motif in which each half corresponds to a head-/tail-end unit, and the central bar becomes the connecting serpent body form. However, each half is also composed of three elements: two heads/tails (the wings, a–c or c–a) and a central unit (the bird head, b). This pattern is perhaps seen more clearly in Figs. 34 and 92. Here a and c within each half are separated by a panel outlined with the same color used to identify the serpent in the plate's central bar (B). Each hemispheric half itself comprises a double-headed or head-end–equals–tail-end serpent motif in which a and c as head-/tail-ends are conjoined by panel b as the serpent body form. However, the overall plate design also presents a double-headed form (the two hemispheres A and A as head-ends) conjoined by a serpent body form (the central bar, B) (see also Figs. 52, 93, 50, 54, and 16; Lothrop 1976:106 top r., 41 bottom r.).

It is intriguing to consider what we might find if plates such as these, depicting both a central panel separating the hemispheres and a panel central to each half, were viewed with the two halves folded up at the

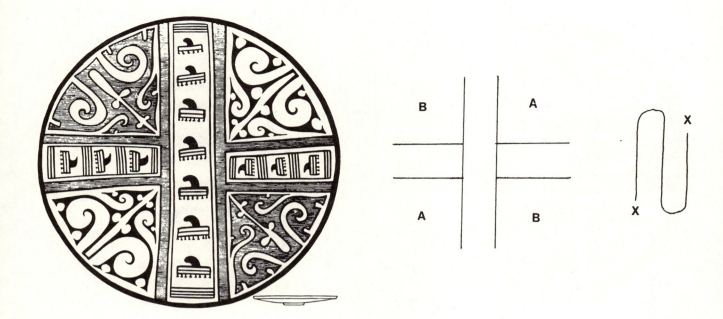

center (Fig. 94) In this perspective the side panels become upright vertical panels, suggesting correlation with the World Tree. The bases of these vertical panels, or world pillars, then touch the center of the horizontal panel, which may designate another cosmological coordinate. The side panels and central panel together could readily delineate the multiple vertical and horizontal dimensions that constitute cosmological space-time overall.

In another variety of whole-plate design the basic design style involves an element in the center of the plate—sometimes a circle—and four elements dividing the rest of the plate into quadrants. A version of this design style was encountered above in the depictions of central circles containing (possibly) cacao beans with spokes or panels radiating out to the rim of the plate so as to delineate four equal quadrants (e.g., Fig. 82). However, there are numerous other designs in which this basic format is modified so that each pair of opposite quadrants (A and C) contains similar or identical elements contrasting with those contained in the other quadrant pair (B and B), which are identical (Figs. 95 and 96; see also Fig. 84; Lothrop 1976:5 top r., 14 bottom l.).

This format is essentially identical to that used in depictions of front-facing standing figures with waist-dependent creatures on gold chest plaques (Figs. 79 and 80), in which quadrants A and C delineate the above-waist and below-waist portions of the figure, while quadrants B and B delineate the waist-dependent creatures—Fig. 95(b). Here it is important to note that quadrants A and C form a continuum with the central circle. That is, the circle and the quadrants form the body of the standing figure, while the B quadrants contain elements attached or

FIG. 93(a). *Whole-plate design format expressing double-headed motif in abstract designs. The two dark quadrants, as head-ends, are conjoined by the contrastive color used to depict the other quadrants and panels. From Lothrop (1976:40).*

FIG. 93(b). *Schematic rendering of format of Fig. 93(a).*

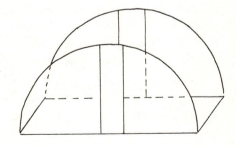

FIG. 94. *Hemispheric whole-plate design formats imagined as expressing multiple horizontal and vertical space-time dimensions or axes.*

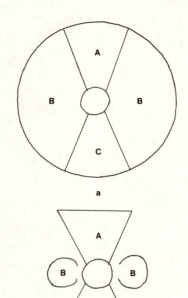

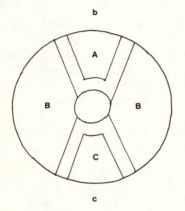

FIG. 95. *Above: Quadripartite whole-plate design formats (a) and (c) compared with chest plaque formats (b).*

FIG. 96. *Above, right: Quadripartite whole-plate design format in which top and bottom quadrants, linked by color to the central circle (and perhaps representing two boa rectangles joined by a boa oval) form one connected unit (a section or boa) corresponding to the standing figures on the gold plaques, while the mammalian beings in the side quadrants are separate, comparable to the waist-dependent iguanas on the gold plaques. From Lothrop (1976:14).*

related to, but not inherent in, the standing figure. This design format is also sometimes seen in Coclé ceramic pieces (Figs. 63 and 67; see also Lothrop 1976:59 top) in depictions that are perhaps less immediately obvious.[1] In Fig. 67, for example, the format seems to leave the center empty, defines the A and C "body" quadrants in terms of the identical heads of two serpents, and defines the two B quadrants in terms of identical mammalian forms positioned as tail-ends of each of the serpents but located at what would be waist level. In Fig. 63 the side or B quadrants are abstract in shape and the central area is the space between the feet of the two female forms facing each other as quadrants A and C.

This general design format is also seen in Fig. 10 (see also Lothrop 1976:49 top l.), which was previously interpreted as representing a close-up of a boa oval (the circle containing a creature) flanked by portions of adjacent boa rectangles. The boa oval now appears as comparable to the central circle, and the two adjacent rectangular sections stand as quadrants A and C—see Figs. 95(c) and 96. Again it is noteworthy that the circle and rectangles form part of a continuous form (a section of boa), comparable in that sense with the standing figures on the gold plaques—Fig. 95(b) and suggestive of Fig. 96. In Fig. 10 the side ("waist") or B quadrants are now occupied by identical birds that are presumably related thematically in some manner to the boa, though they are not directly attached to (that is, not inherently part of) the boa form (compare the waist-dependent animals on the gold plaques and the side quadrant mammalian forms on Fig. 96).

Within the broader context of "whole-plate designs" the possibility should be considered that meaning was also encoded in the forms in which the ceramic pieces were shaped. This point is obvious when effigy forms are involved, but the dual hemispheres of a globular carafe or the simple circularity of a plate or bowl may have conveyed cosmological significance, too. For example, a Kuna description of the eight layers of the heavens notes that the eighth and final layer takes the form of a pottery vessel (Nordenskiöld 1979:157–158), while the depiction of the Talamancan universe in Fig. 98 depicts a pottery vessel covering the peak of the cosmic "house," just as an old ceramic pot was placed over the peak opening of the traditional Talamancan conical house to keep out the rain.

Similarly, Reichel-Dolmatoff, speaking of the Desana, describes how the cooking vessels and large circular earthenware manioc griddle represent the Creation, part of the symbolism of fertility associated with the hearth as "an instrument of cosmic transformation, a crucible" (Reichel-Dolmatoff 1971:108; see also Pauketat and Emerson 1991:931–934). Such an interpretation falls within the general concept, widespread in the Americas, that containers of all sorts, including (among other things) houses, boxes, and dishes as well as the human body, hold or are occupied by cosmological "vital forces" (e.g., Goldman 1975:64). Ceramic pieces in particular may be especially apt vehicles for "containments" and expressions of this sort because the process of crafting a firmly shaped ceramic piece from formless malleable clay is one of the most fundamental expressions of transformation known to, and practised by, humans, often considered comparable to the creation of human life itself.[2] In this sense ceramics become fundamentally symbolic by the very mode of their formation (Lévi-Strauss 1988:177–178, 18–19, 21).

In light of these points, it seems reasonable to suggest that the overall shape accorded Coclé ceramic pieces—trays, plates, bowls, carafes, and pedestal bases—also encoded meaning. For example, consider the carafe, seemingly composed of two hemispheres meeting in the middle at a sharply delineated edge or curve and with a central cylindrical neck (Fig. 97; see also Lothrop 1976:52–53). This form suggests the type of whole-plate design composed of two halves separated by a central panel or bar (in the carafe the central bar is represented by the center plane where the two hemispherical halves meet). The overall globular or dual hemisphere shape of the carafe also suggests the "conical" cosmos as envisioned in Talamancan cosmology, where multiple cosmic layers of underworld and heaven, respectively, extend in planes of

FIG. 97. *Carafe suggesting in its shape the dual hemisphere motif of some plates and/or a conical cosmos with the neck of the carafe as axis mundi. From Lothrop (1976:53).*

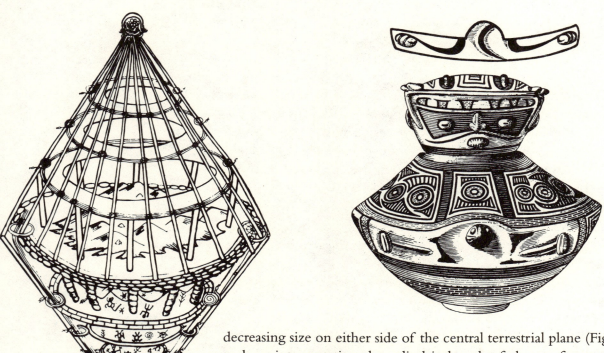

FIG. 98. *The cosmos as two cones meeting at the central terrestrial plane as interpreted in Talamancan cosmology. From González and González (1989:146, Fig. 24). By permission of Universidad Estatal a Distancia.*

FIG. 99. *Effigy carafe representing a sea turtle. From Lothrop (1976:62).*

decreasing size on either side of the central terrestrial plane (Fig. 98). In such an interpretation the cylindrical neck of the carafe can easily be seen to represent an axis mundi.

Some of the carafes in effigy forms invite further reflection. In addition to those discussed above as possible snuffing jars and depicting various reptiles, fish, and mammals, others (e.g., Fig. 99) are clearly modeled and painted as sea turtles sometimes combining the body of the carafe-as-turtle with a seemingly humanoid head. Until relatively recently great numbers of female sea turtles annually crawled from the sea, at night, onto the beaches of Central America (some still do), each intent on excavating a nest in the sand and laying a cache of eggs (Carr 1967). Such creatures from the sea nesting on the littoral would have been redolent with cosmological import probably signifying transformation, liminality, origins, and fertility. The frequent rendering of the cover of the neck of the vessel as a humanoid head which appears to emerge from the turtle's back when the cover is in place (Fig. 99; cf. Lothrop 1976:61–62) brings to mind Mayan depictions of the emergence of the Maize God, First Father, from a cracked turtle carapace (Freidel, Schele, and Parker 1993:65, 94, 281–282).

Turning to circular plates, the circularity of such wares in and of itself may have had significance, perhaps designating the boa oval/circle. In ritual use such a circular container might have "become" the serpent and the physical materials it held (perhaps cacao or plant hallucinogens or other ritual paraphernalia)[3] could have taken on potencies associated with qualities of the serpent. Such plates and their contents might have served as unifying or communication media relating human participants

to the realms of the cosmos (cf. Reichel-Dolmatoff 1972:89–90). Richard Cooke's identification of the multicolored rim of some Panamanian (Macaracas-style) vessels as representative of the serpent is very appropriate within this context, too (Cooke 1985:38, 39; see also rims on Figs. 16, 20, and 76).

Additional hints of the possible significance of ceramic circularity may be found in the symbolism associated with circular house construction by Talamancan peoples. Here the completeness of the circle is related to the spiral, the serpent, and planetary paths (González and González 1989:14). Possibly the circular plate also related to the earth as a disk; Talamancans view the earth as a great disk surrounded by the sea (González and González 1989:152).

Alternatively, any circular plate design involving a central circle surrounded by one or more concentric bands (Fig. 100; see also Lothrop 1976:27 top r.) could express a "collapsed" interpretation of a circular or conically shaped cosmos composed of various circular planes or levels and a central unifying axis mundi (Fig. 98). Pursuing this type of cosmological interpretation, the cylindrical pedestal base on which plates sometimes sit may have referred to (or represented) some form of axis mundi. We may wonder, too, whether the complete ensemble of vessel shapes and sizes, in its entirety and apart from the functionality of shape alone, addressed a diversity-in-totality theme with cosmological and sociological relevance (David, Sterner, and Gavua 1988:367–370).

Cosmology may also have been referenced on the Coclé polychrome ceramics by the application of brilliance or luminosity. This quality is widely recognized in traditional societies worldwide as a highly valued

FIG. 100. *Multiple nested circles with central point and surrounding serpent Y-element kennings. Design may represent a "collapsed" portrayal of a conical universe with multiple layers or levels surrounding an axis mundi. From Lothrop (1976:21).*

aesthetic element. It is accorded to many types of natural and crafted things associated with special personal, social or ceremonial statuses or events. Brilliance or luminosity is manifested in the polish given by artisans to stone, metal, or wood, in the shine of mirrors, and in the glazes applied to ceramics.[4] It is recognized as a quality of the natural world, too, appearing in the sparkle of water, the rays of the sun, the rainbow-like iridescence of animal pelts, birds' feathers, and the scales of reptiles, and the wetness of potters' clay.

Luminosity was also applied to the polychrome pottery of Sitio Conte. According to Lothrop (who also commented on the wide distribution of polished or glazed ceramic wares in the Americas in general),

almost all polychrome pottery in the ground is very lustrous, but if the surface is touched even with a brush the shine will disappear. ... At the Sitio Conte we were unable to preserve it. This apparently indicates that the vessels received a definite coating of some kind. [1942:12]

Lothrop suggests that some sort of vegetal substance rather like a varnish was used (cf. Whitten and Whitten 1988:20).

Judging from ethnographic evidence, the quality of luminosity relates to celestial phenomena, light and brightness, the presence of supernatural energy, health and well-being, and ancestral origins. It may be evoked both in the actual appearances of things, either crafted or in their natural state, and in the emotional response induced in viewers or celebrants, whose reaction may be interpreted as an aesthetic expression signifying the presence of ancestral power (Morphy 1989; Morphy 1991:193–196). Among the Desana, the color concept of "white," which essentially refers to energy, also encodes the quality of brilliance and stands opposed to "dullness" (Reichel-Dolmatoff 1978:256–259). According to Roe,

As part of a sophisticated dualism, South Amerindians distinguish between luminance and chroma. Something that is light and bright, i.e., reflective, should be aligned with the Upper World of the light, bright and reflective Sun. A color that is dark and dull should be identified with the somber hues of the Lower World and the Moon. However, even something that is dark, but reflective through the property of iridescence, can be "bright" and hence classified with the other bright "light" colors. Conversely, a dull "light" color becomes classified with the "dark" dull colors. [1989:13–14]

Roe goes on to note how, among the Shipibo, the skin of the anaconda in its coloration and in its iridescence not only is associated with darkness (the darkness of its green and black markings) but also with "brightness" (the shimmering aspect of the scales) and thus with the celestial realm. In the context of the light and the celestial, the anaconda relates to the "Celestial Dragon" (Feathered Serpent) whose "lightness" is manifested both in the rainbow and when, by its (presumably shining) blood, it gives bright colors to birds (Roe 1989:14, 15).

Given the proposed serpent-related and color-related thematic content of much of the Coclé polychrome designs as well as evidence that the entire surface of the wares was originally accorded "brilliance," it is probable that the quality of luminosity was recognized and accorded cosmological meanings in ancient Panama, too. It is particularly interesting in this respect to note that boas, especially after shedding, show a particularly marked iridescence of the skin—a zoological characteristic that would readily relate luminosity with origins or new birth or immortality in cosmological thought (Schmidt and Inger 1957:177). The gleam of the tinamou egg could well have carried comparable association, too. I also suggest that the quality of brilliance may be expressed stylistically in Panamanian ceramic art when portions of designs are outlined with a thin dark line marked with small dots or short lines (e.g., Figs. 47, 15, 24, 39). The brilliance of gleaming gold was also ubiquitous in ancient Panamanian ornamentation, and it is a common marker in contemporary Kuna myths and chants as well.

CONCLUDING REMARKS

The Coclé polychrome ceramics were crafted a thousand years ago, and interpretations of the meanings of design motifs and the thematic metaphors they encode must remain provisional. Nonetheless, the richness and sophistication of the Coclé designs and the wealth of themes they suggest clearly place this art squarely within the great corpus of native American art, myth, and symbolism in general. In addition, both design forms and suggested symbolism invite explicit comparison with this same body of traditional native American thought and expression. Although it has not been my intent in this work to pursue cross-cultural comparisons with any degree of rigor or thoroughness, various comparisons have been made when particularly appropriate. Many more have not been pursued, but it seems reasonable to conclude in general that the Coclé ceramic art addresses sociological, cosmological, and cosmogonical themes widespread in the Americas, indeed worldwide.

These themes appear to be extremely ancient and are quite variable cross-culturally in terms of the particulars of their expressions. However, they often retain an astonishing consistency in the types of structural relations expressed among constituent thematic units and in the basic issues addressed. These include such universal concerns as immortality versus death, the place and role of human existence among the diversity of life forms of sky, earth, and sea, the origins of such diversity and of human life, the awesome power of the cosmic forces held responsible for original creations and their continued regeneration, the continued expression of these fundamental forces in the world of nature, and the dynamics and periodicities of the realms of the sky, earth and waters. Equally fundamental questions, also universally addressed, concern relationships within and between human societies as expressed by kinship and affinity, admonishment and obedience and the nature of Us versus Others.

Such sociological concerns are often accorded validation by reference to the dynamics of the wider cosmos. They are frequently expressed metaphorically, however, by reference to characteristics of life forms of nature. In this context the following statement by Reichel-Dolmatoff concerning the Tukanoans of Northwest Amazonia is an essential methodological reminder:

It is true that shamans do talk and sing a lot about animals and to animals and that animals figure very prominently in their ideology and practice. However, ... all this preoccupation with animals is not concerned with the zoological species and their economic importance but with their symbolic value. At times, shamans become quite annoyed if someone gives too much weight to the mere biological and economic aspects and will unequivocally insist on the semantic value of animals. Animals are images, they will say, that represent abstract concepts in a cognitive system which includes all of nature and which in the last resort, goes far beyond it. [Reichel-Dolmatoff 1985:140]

It would probably be foolhardy to attempt to identify too many abstract concepts and equally misleading to focus too heavily on specific zoological identifications in a body of (to us) anonymously created pre-Columbian art like that of Coclé since too much reconstruction would easily slip into excessive speculation. Nevertheless, attempts to identify the more readily recognizable zoological species and recognition of at least general similarities between Coclé design forms and possible thematic motifs and those of other native American cultures appear both warranted and intellectually safe (e.g., Helms 1992). The fundamental role of the serpent in Coclé ceramic art is a case in point. Surely this portrayal of the serpent motif can be interpreted as a variant within the virtually worldwide expression[1] of serpent lore which, in general, reflects metaphors of dynamic power, generativity (sexuality, reproduction), cultural and human origins, transformation from the shapeless void of the primordial to formal, organized and processual cultural life, the need for logical and sociological differentiations between categories of self and others and, sometimes, aspects of leadership (Drummond 1981).

Within such a general setting the Coclé serpent also shares more specific representational and stylistic formats with other expressions of the serpent motif. For example, in Coclé art, as we have seen, the serpent frequently composes a fundamental part of the body form of other creatures, which can thereby be viewed as composite in form. Such representations parallel the role of the serpent in the composition of the "fabulous beast" described for Ilama ceramic art (Western Colombia) by Schrimpff (1989:79–98; see also Labbé 1986:54–55) and the various feathered, plumed and horned serpents of Mesoamerica and North America (Miller and Taube 1993:148–151, 141). Barbeau, for example, describes a composite serpent-deer of the Iroquoian Wyandot tribe of the Great Lakes of North America with attributes that in many ways suggest Fig. 90 of the Coclé art: "a head surmounted by a pair of pronged deer horns, a cavernous mouth with serrated teeth breathing deadly fumes and flames, large rolling eyes, a huge body covered with fish scales shining like polished brass, a reptilian tail..." (Barbeau 1967:116).

Similarly, the double-headed serpent is paralleled in the Sisiutl, the two-headed sea serpent of the Northwest Coast, which is often depicted as a central face with human features and spiral horns flanked on either side by a snake body and head, also with a spiral head crest or horn (cf. Fig. 39) (Stewart 1979:70–71; see also southeastern Mississippian serpent depictions in Brown 1985:123–126; Penney 1985:180, 185, 189–194). It is also widespread in Andean iconography, often as a great double-headed serpentine arch interpreted as rainbow-, sky-, and rain-related (Carlson 1982). Among the Classic Maya the double-headed serpent bar is associated with the World Tree and symbol of kingship (Schele and Miller 1986:72; Schele and Freidel 1990:68–69, 415–416, 418; Bassie-Sweet 1991:chap. 4), while the double-headed serpent as vision serpent appears in Maya bloodletting ritual (Schele and Miller 1986:46–47, 177, 187–188) and as representative of the ecliptic (that is, as the path of the sun and the planets and the way along which supernaturals traveled en route to this world) (Freidel, Schele, and Parker 1993:78–79, 196).

It is, of course, impossible to know with certainty whether or not the Coclé serpent motif also referenced the rainbow and related concepts of chromatics, but given the wide distribution of such themes in relation to the serpent and the evidence that the qualities of light (brilliance) and polychromatics were accorded to Coclé ceramics, such associations seem plausible. Within contemporary indigenous Central American cosmology the possible association of the Coclé serpent with the rainbow is encouraged by a Talamancan tale which identifies the rainbow with an enormous serpent that lives in lagoons (Bozzoli de Wille and Cubero 1988:84, 86; see also Conzemius 1932:169 regarding beliefs by indigenous peoples of the Miskito Coast about a giant boa associated with thunder and lightning that inhabits large lagoons and swallows unwary intruders).

In addition, some of the solar-related serpent themes discussed in this work, particularly those relating to creation or coloration by blood (which also involved the severed leg and perhaps the mythical tailed sloth, too), seem to appear in clearly analogous contexts in Kuna texts in which the color of blood or blood itself determines the type of animal created. In these tales, however, it is the color of the menstrual blood of the Great Mother that determines the identity of the animals she bears[2] while blood from some of the umbilical cords (a seemingly serpentine theme) associated with these births created various birds and fowls and large animals (Nordenskiöld 1979:385–386, 443).[3]

It also seems possible that certain observations by Tacon (with reference to indigenous Australia) might have some relevance for isthmian (and other native American) cosmology, too. Tacon notes that the color animating skin or flesh that living creatures exhibit quickly fades at death. He points out that this phenomenon is particularly pronounced in cold-blooded creatures such as fish or reptiles, where the iridescent rainbow colors of skin and scale change noticeably soon after death, fading to a dull grey. "As a consequence, the presence of color, especially of rainbow colours, has become associated with life and things that are alive while its absence is associated with death" (Tacon 1989:245).

If the Coclé polychrome ceramics with their bright varnish encoded such themes as the dynamics of life, the power of generativity, and cultural origins and transformations, it is understandable that such artistic expressions, and the skilled artisans who crafted them, were also associated with elites. I believe it is likely that from the perspective of elites one of the most important themes encoded in the polychrome designs was the emphasis on creatures and mythemes—the serpent, tinamou, curassow, sloth, perhaps the spectacled bear, the Tree of Life, severed leg, luminosity—that related mythically or metaphorically to origins, creations, or beginnings. Association with, and knowledge about, times and conditions of cosmological and/or cultural origins and creations is a major preoccupation of political and religious authorities in traditional societies because association with origins, with beginnings, both legit-imizes authority and creates personal political ability. Nordenskiöld expresses this very clearly in discussing the importance of a knowledge of origins for Kuna curers:

The Cuna Indians speak most of all about God as the creator of everything. Their art of healing is based on the creation of myths. At the incantations they always go back to a creature's or an objects' [sic] origin and this they find through learning to know how the thing in question was created by God, whether it hap-pens to be a medicinal plant, a stone, a bird, or something else. The strength in the incantation when it for example has to do with a medicine, lies in one's knowing how God created this medicine. It is by knowing how God made the snakes that one can tame them. It is by knowing how God created the protecting spirits, nuchus, that one can include them to help a sick person against the evil spirits. [Nordenskiöld 1979:432–433]

In like fashion Kuna village chiefs, in their political oratory, focus heav-ily on, or take as point of departure, the activities of Great Father and Great Mother, who created the world; Tat Ibe (the sun) and Ipeorkun, two major culture-heroes who introduced vital elements of Kuna cul-ture; and other creational beings or hero personages both from Chris-tianity and from the national history of Colombia and Panama (Howe 1986:chap. 2, chap. 3).

Not only did Coclé ceramics probably relate elites to origins and cre-ations thematically, but it is likely that these wares were used in rituals that effected communication between the human world—especially that of elites—and the spiritual realm.[4] Some also accompanied elites into that realm at death, for it is from discovery of buried ceramics, interred in quantity with deceased lords or in separate caches, that we know of the existence of pre-Columbian Panamanian ceramic art.

Given the hierarchical nature of the pre-Columbian Panamanian societies in question, it is very likely that deceased elites were believed destined to be transformed into ancestors. Hence, it is also possible that burying quantities of elaborately designed polychromed ceramics (along with other elite accoutrements) was thought in some manner to facilitate this transformation, not only by heralding the high status and social identity of the deceased or providing materials for a comfortable afterlife but also, and perhaps most important, by literally identifying and creating a functioning ancestor. Morphy, speaking of the Australian

Yolngu, offers some ideas that may be helpful in understanding how this transformation occurs (see also Helms 1993a:140–145). He explains how painted designs contain the power of ancestral being and how ancestral power is ensured or maintained by returning the power of the deceased to spiritual sources via mortuary rites (1991:102, 105–106). The performance of these rites requires preparation of paintings in association with the body of the dead which assist in the transformation of the soul of the dead into ancestral substance (ibid.:108, 113–114).

Paintings accomplish this transformation in part by visually depicting essential sacred themes and esoteric knowledge (Morphy 1991). Campbell also recounts how the act of writing, meaning the creation of designs, including those painted on the body, incised into pottery, and found on the bodies of anacondas and jaguars, was seen by the Wayapí of Brazil as a means of creating and recording knowledge: "The act of writing is diagnostic as well as mnemonic" (1989:59). Surely the designs painted on Coclé ceramic pieces encoded (brought into tangible being) sacred themes and knowledge, too: presumably knowledge of the form, meaning, mechanisms, and powers of the cosmos and its powerful supernatural agents and of the place and relationships of human society therein. Ancestors in the afterworld, like their still-living elite counterparts, presumably were regarded as essential agents through whom such knowledge, and thus spiritual power, could be ritually accumulated and then reactivated for the benefit of human social living. Encapsulating such knowledge and power in a tangible form by painting the appropriate representations on ceramic pieces presumably assisted its ritual preservation and activation. In like fashion the burial of such ceramic wares with deceased elites returned this valuable knowledge and dynamic generative power to the cosmological realm together with the earthly remains of the beings who, as ancestors, would be responsible for making it available once again (through ritual) for human use. In short, burying polychrome ceramics and other ideologically potent materials (e.g., gold ornaments) with elites may have been an important step guaranteeing literally both the continued revitalization of cosmological life and the creation of functioning ancestors (Helms 1993a:142–145).

The creation of functioning ancestors may have been facilitated further by the purposeful destruction of some mortuary ceramics. Lothrop notes (see Preface above) that pottery vessels at the Sitio Conte were frequently "killed" by trampling, "reduc[ing] complete vessels to a compacted and intermingled mass of sherds" that often resulted in ceramic layers several inches thick (1942:3–5). I suggest that this trampling may have been accomplished during mortuary rites by ceremonial dancing at the burial site. We have encountered seemingly destructive ceremonial dancing before in the Talamancan creation myth describing how a child was trampled during a dance (Chapter 6). In this tale the mangled remains of the crushed child becomes the fertile earth that is populated by plants, animals, and people.

Talamancan beliefs also specify direct correspondences between ceramics and human beings. In an origin tale, major deities of the underworld (the Surá) are described as potters who also create human beings. In addition, the life of a clay vessel is compared to the life of a human being and damage to a clay vessel is seen as similar to human illness, both being reparable sometimes but not always (González and González 1989:123–124, 158; cf. Helms 1993b:244). It is noteworthy, too, that both human beings and ceramic wares are decorated with paint and ultimately, it would appear, both humans and pottery vessels share a common final fate since both eventually "break" and "die."

If this Talamancan correspondence between ceramics and humans is extended to the Sitio Conte burials it is easy to understand why ceramics would be "killed" by being trampled under dancing feet at the deaths of human beings, especially elites. Conceivably, too, the crushing ("sacrifice") of polychrome ceramics at such times, releasing the power encapsulated in painted designs and ceramic forms, was believed to facilitate the creation of renewed cosmic life for the deceased as beneficent ancestors, whose powers would assist plants, animals, and people to flourish in the earthly realm just as the remains of the sacrificial child in the Talamancan myth created the fertile earth and readied the world for people, plants, and animals. The message seems clear: from the chaos, disorder and formlessness evoked by death and destruction, be it expressed by a trampled child, a lifeless elite or broken pottery, comes both promise and means for a return to order and renewed life.[5]

In the introduction to this work, reference was made to Alice in Wonderland's bemusement at a book without pictures. We may regard with comparable bemusement a mode of communication, such as the Coclé polychrome ceramics, based entirely on pictures. It is important to remember, however, that the two are not entirely comparable modes of communication. We can assume that (paraphrasing Isadora Duncan)[6] if the messages contained in the Coclé designs were the sorts of messages that could have been adequately conveyed in words alone, there would have been no point in painting them. Consequently, any attempt to decode these messages, these metaphors, with words and especially to do so across a wide span of time and cultural difference certainly must include some degree of error and incompleteness. Nonetheless, such efforts seem warranted if we may gain at least a small glimpse into the world of thought and wisdom systematically expressed a thousand years ago by a distinctive style of design and truly masterful artistic skill (Bateson 1972). At the very least we can deepen our appreciation of, and respect for, the wonderful sophistication with which it was done.

CONCLUDING REMARKS

NOTES

INTRODUCTION

1. Ability as a master craftsman may be one of the qualities sought in potential leaders. For example, see Fernandez (1973:207–209, 219); Tuzin (1978); Rabineau (1975).

CHAPTER 1: CHROMATICS

1. In using mythemes and ethnographic materials from South America as a guide to elucidate certain characteristics of Panamanian ceramics, I am not asserting that Panamanian ceramic styles per se derived from South America.

2. Eco (1986:50), speaking of Medieval Europe, talks of similar concepts in which color-filled jewels from the earth are believed to be solidified portions of the celestial color spectrum as it hit the earth, in other words, congealed sunlight.

3. In the context of astronomy, in much of Amazonia the great serpent is also widely associated with Scorpius (Hugh-Jones 1982:190–191).

4. Among the Miskito and Sumu people of the Miskito Coast of eastern Nicaragua the rainbow is the representative of the god of wind and air who sends destructive hurricanes and floods. When the rainbow appeared, Indians are said to have hidden their children so that they would not see or point at it; if pointed at, it is believed that the outstretched hand or arm will become crippled and covered with terrible sores (Conzemius 1932:126–127). According to Nordenskiöld (1979:394) the Kuna of Panama had the same belief about the dangers of pointing at the rainbow.

5. The dual themes of conjunctive (rain-related) and disjunctive (sun-related) rainbow/serpents correlate clearly both with the highland Mesoamerican duality of the feathered serpent as conjoining earth and sky and as harbinger of the rainy season and the destructive fire serpent as harbinger of

the dry season, and with the Chacs of the lowland Maya, strongly snake-associated and also believed capable of both sending and withholding rain (Thompson 1970:253).

6. In comparable fashion, the patterns on the skin of a giant snake were the inspiration for designs woven into basketry and beadwork and, apparently, painted onto the human body among various peoples of lowland South America (Howard 1991:55; Roe 1989:14, 18–20, 22, 32, 34; Campbell 1989:59, 82). It should be noted, too, that a portion of a Kuna (Panama) text tells how the culture-hero, Ibeorgun, passed on information to the people about a woman who had discovered plant dyes and different colored clays to be used in making pottery (Nordenskiöld 1979:135).

CHAPTER 2: THE SERPENT

1. It is interesting that dancing, in conjunction with mangled flesh, creates the fertile earth in Talamancan myth. See chapter 6.

2. A kenning is an artistic device in which identification of, or comparison with, something is made by substitution of something else (Rowe 1962, 1967: 77–82).

3. It may be noted, too, that boas bear their own young live.

4. The range of the resplendent quetzal (*Pharomachrus mocinno*), famed for its extraordinary train of tail feathers, extends to western Panama. The golden-headed quetzal (*Pharomachrus auriceps*), with much shorter tail, is found in eastern Panama and adjacent northern South America (Ridgely and Gwynne 1989:228–229).

5. Compare the modes of depiction of the giant serpents associated with Chacs from the Codex Madrid as shown on Plates 9 and 10 in Thompson (1970), where the serpents are portrayed in very clear Y-element positions (actually more U-shaped with a tail).

6. Possibly the boa's loud hiss was part of its symbolic value. Aural effects, including buzzing or whirring sounds, have been related to hallucinogenic experiences in a number of cultures, worldwide, and are sometimes deliberately produced in rituals by bullroarers (Whitley 1993:5, 14, 15).

7. Lothrop (1976:96 top l., 97 top r.) depicts rows of crosses +++++ on container rims which may be kennings for the emerald tree boa (*Boa canina*), a striking green snake with a row of strongly delineated white or yellow crosses down its back (Schmidt and Inger 1957:177).

CHAPTER 3: BIRDS AND FOWL

1. Talamancan peoples of southern Costa Rica also identify such "eagles" as buzzards, the earthly form taken by their prime deity, Sibu (Stone 1967:252, 1962:70).

2. Cracids are also very sociable, with strong pair or group associations.

They shelter their young by protectively taking a chick under each wing on the roost. Cracids are also easily tamed and have long been kept domestically by indigenous tribes, including peoples of Panama (Delacour and Amadon 1973:13, 16, Fig. 8, 73; Bennett 1968:49).

3. In Huichol art, depiction of the internal parts—specifically the skeletal bones—of an animal, such as a deer, relates to the belief that life resides in the bones and that the animal will be reborn from its skeletal parts (Berrin 1978:160; see also chapter 6, note 4 and the discussion of cacao seeds below). In Coclé art the same theme may have been expressed by way of an internal serpentine motif. See also Lévi-Strauss's discussion of the significance of viscera in myths (1973:263–266, 1969:243–246).

4. Wetmore records a local folktale from Panama which, though it has an obvious Christian context, also seems to be related to, though structurally the reverse of, this account: "… when the Rainbow of Promise appeared in the sky following the Flood [as opposed to the World Fire], the brilliant colors so frightened the *perdiz* [great tinamou] that it flew out in terror from the company of other birds in the Ark of Noah [as opposed to seeking shelter within a vessel] to shelter in the forest …" (Wetmore 1965:9; parenthetical comments mine). In Kuna tales from Panama shelter is provided to a few fortunate well-behaved people by a big clay vessel, buried upside down in the earth, where they hid and survived the great darkness that destroyed an evil world (Nordenskiöld 1979:261, 263, 274, 436).

5. According to some Indian tales, in the tropical night sky the severed leg can be seen in the constellation we know as Orion's Belt (Lévi-Strauss 1969:110, 225, 221, Fig. 11).

6. For the Shipibo, however, the dull-colored, slow-moving terrestrial tinamou is opposed to bright-colored, high-flying, solar (celestial) birds, such as the harpy eagle (Roe 1988:126). The tinamou also was one of the two birds that survived the great drought that destroyed the evil of the world in Desana myth (Reichel-Dolmatoff 1971:34).

7. See Lothrop (1976:102 top r.), which, however, could just as easily be a guan, perhaps the Cauca guan (*Penelope perspicax*) (Delacour and Amadon 1973:1350).

CHAPTER 4: MAMMALS

1. In Lothrop (1976:100 l., 2nd from top) a bird effigy figure, suggesting a nightjar, a type of bird (*Caprimulgidae*) mentioned in South American myth (e.g., Lévi-Strauss 1973:126) is depicted with "digits" rather than claws. Another possibility is that the "paws" seen in Figs. 69 and 70 might instead represent bivalved shells (especially Fig. 69), since the number of "digits" in each pair neatly interdigitates.

2. In the words of a Spanish colonial monk, Antonio de la Calancha, "The Indians of the Andes, who live in the lands behind snow-capped mountains,

where it always rains and where it is very hot … , and the Indians who live in the mountains, worship Tigers, Lions, Bears, and Serpents, because there is an abundance of these species in their countries" (qtd. in Zuidema 1985:234).

3. The spectacled bear is also an important animal in myth and symbolism in the southern part of its range; see Gilmore (1950:376), Urton (1985:270–272), and note 2.

4. Note the association of bear and jaguar again; two of the most powerful of the Andean and tropical lowland animals.

5. See also the hunter who can transform into a bear and the less obvious association between a probable bear and a young man transformed into a woman in Sibundoy Valley tales (McDowell 1989:111–112). The Desana female culture heroine, the Daughter of the Sun, comes to mind, too (Reichel-Dolmatoff 1971:28–29, 35). Although it is far afield, the concept of the Lady of Wild Things or Mistress of the Animals, also associated with the bear, found in ancient Hellenic tradition, comes to mind, too (Ripinsky-Naxon 1993:31–33).

6. To the extent that bear motifs and bird motifs may appear related in Coclé ceramic art, it is interesting that symbolic association between birds and bears involving rain and weather or seasonality or associating birds as souls of the dead with the bear as guardian of the underworld are found in various cultures (Shepard and Sanders 1985:65–66). Apparently, too, in some traditional cultures in Asia and North America bears as primordial creators of landscape are associated with color and with the grinders and whetstones necessary to prepare pigments; the bear as a curer par excellence exhaled colored dusts from its nostrils or spat colored dirt from its mouth. The color red is said to come from the blood of the animal and black from its excrement (Shepard and Sanders 1985:73, 101).

7. The mythical *boráro* is also said to wear a colored headdress of feathers (Reichel-Dolmatoff 1975:187).

8. The central figure on the gold plaques (Figs. 79 and 80) may be associated in contemporary Kuna myths with Tad Ibe, a culture-hero who has solar affinities and is also related to the iguana. The depictions of these broad-headed central figures on gold plaques, however, also indicate human teeth combined with plantigrade but clawed paws, suggesting a human-animal transformation theme. The question of whether this central figure is related to the bear, as suggested by the broad head and plantigrade paws, or to the iguana, as suggested by the Panamanian myth, may be mooted to some extent by the two fragments of myth mentioned above from Colombia and from Panama, respectively, in which the bear and the iguana carry the same structural role. In addition, at the end of the Panamanian myth the iguana, in defeat, is transformed from a supernatural protagonist into an edible earthly form. To recognize the central hunter or Master of Animals as a bear-human carrying edible iguanas as game seems to reconcile the mythemes very nicely.

9. On the subject of spectacles, Lévi-Strauss comments on the intense

interest that South American Indians showed in spectacles, "so much so that on my last expedition I took along a great quantity of glassless spectacle-frames. These had a great success among the Nambikwara. ..." He notes the ceremonial dress of the Bororo, which at times included "what looked like a huge pair of glassless straw spectacles around [the performer's] eyes," and comments briefly upon the eye motif of the Mesoamerican god of rain, Tlaloc, and concepts of Pueblo peoples associating eyes with invisibility, rain, and the dead (Lévi-Strauss 1964:226).

10. It is noteworthy that monkeys were associated with the arts, including painting, writing, music and dance, by the Classic Maya (Baker 1992).

CHAPTER 5: THE TREE OF LIFE AND ITS PRODUCTS

1. It is interesting, too, that the four panels from central circle to plate edge in Fig. 82 are rectangular, perhaps corresponding to the boa rectangles. This idea may be strengthened by the serpentine-related double-headed motif indicated by the Y-elements composing these panels.

2. These contents include the waters and life forms within the hollow trunk, the serpent's blood, and cacao beans inside the pod.

3. See also chapter 6, note 4, which suggests a possible correlation between the cacao and other tree seed and the severed limb (as bone correlating with ancestors) motif.

4. The same idea may be expressed in the small pendants found at Sitio Conte composed "internally" of ivory (whale tooth), bone (deer or manatee), or molded or carved plant resin—all probably value-laden materials (see note 6 regarding the resin)—which were then sheathed in ("contained within") sheet gold (Hearne and Sharer 1992:94–99).

5. Shortly thereafter a tremendous flood destroyed everyone except the serpent and his human family.

6. Virola snuff is prepared from the red resin contained in the bark of several species of tropical forest trees of genus Virola. After stripping the bark and soaking it in cold water, the resin exuding from the bark begins to congeal and can be scraped off. After further processing it is reduced to a powder (Reichel-Dolmatoff 1975:20–21). In note 4 reference is made to small effigy animals from Sitio Conte carefully fashioned of a dark red plant resin and then covered with embossed gold (Hearne and Sharer 1992:99, Plates 29 and 30). As to the styles of the proposed Coclé effigy snuff pots themselves, the positioning of the nosepiece as the animal's tail is found elsewhere (e.g., Furst 1974: 84) and the types of animals depicted include birds, mammals, and reptiles, seeming to expand upon the bird theme frequently associated with ecstatic intoxication in tropical America (Wassén 1965:24–29).

7. Taussig is speaking of yajé visions experienced by Siona people of the Putumayo River region.

CHAPTER 6: BODY PARTS AND PROCESSES

1. In Mayan political-ideology GII is particularly associated with the bloodletting ritual, kingship, and the ancestors and is the god most frequently shown on the double-headed serpent bar (Schele and Freidel 1990:414; Schele and Miller 1986:49; Robicsek 1978:chap. 6, chap. 11). See Concluding Remarks.

2. See also Pressman (1991:85) for a related version involving an eagle, a boy's severed leg, and containers full of blood that changed into different colors of paint with which birds were colored.

3. The severed-leg theme also relates to the rainbow serpent in a number of other contexts not considered here, such as fishing. See Lévi-Strauss (1969:216 and 1968:38–40, 46–50, 106). A bent and shriveled leg is attributed to snake bite in a Barasana myth (Hugh-Jones 1979:145).

4. Bones are widely believed to be the seat of life; "rebirth proceeds as much from one's bones as the life of a tree springs from the hard seed—universally called 'bone' in Mesoamerica—contained within the flesh of a fruit" (Furst 1978:23).

5. Closure, meaning being stopped up or having excessive continence or being imprudent, is expressed by sleep, deafness, dumbness or in various bodily digestive stoppages (Lévi-Strauss 1969:128, 134–135). See discussion of the anteater above.

6. In contemporary Mayan tales the initiation ritual in the creation of a shaman may involve being "swallowed" and then "excreted" by a giant serpent as link or path of communication with the otherworld (Freidel, Schele, and Parker 1993:209, 448, note 74). Conceivably portrayals of the Coclé serpent as double-headed and open-mouthed could contain references to such shamanic transformation.

7. Parallels between the open-mouth motif and the very widespread "dangerous vagina" mytheme would be relevant here, too.

8. There is a similarity in the Kuna terms *nukar,* meaning teeth, and *nuka,* name.

9. Stretched or extended tongues, depicted in various forms of ancient Panamanian iconography, are also mentioned in a series of Kuna stories where they relate to the acquisition of useful plants from the underworld (Hayans 1952:92–94).

CHAPTER 7: WHOLE-PLATE DESIGNS

1. An interesting variation is seen in Lothrop (1976:59 top) where the central "circle" is replaced by the broad toothed mouth, but the head and feet (A and C) of the figure are readily identifiable. The serpent-related forms comprising side "quadrants" (B and B) are attached not to a waist but to the eyes of the figure.

2. See discussion in Helms (1993b:244) regarding comparabilities between the creation and existence of clay vessels and human beings and possible parallels between the decoration of human beings (body painting) and the decoration of ceramics suggested by Talamancan tales.

3. Among the Maya ritual offerings, including strips of paper saturated with blood and perhaps chicle resin, were placed in large plates and carried to braziers, where they were burned to create smoke. In classic Maya depictions bowls containing bloody paper, stingray spines, and lancets are shown as part of the vision stage of the bloodletting rite in which visions conjured ancestors via the medium of the Great Snake (Vision Serpent) (Schele and Miller 1986:178, 187, 190; Schele and Freidel 1990:406, 407).

4. In another portion of the myth concerning the origin of painted earthenware quoted in chapter 1, the snake/sprite who taught the young woman how to craft polychrome ceramics uses a black varnish to decorate and *give lustre to* a number of gourds (Lévi-Strauss 1969:323).

CONCLUDING REMARKS

1. The prominence of the serpent in native systems of belief and representation in Oceania, Africa, Eurasia, the Near East, and the Americas has been well documented. For a sample of this voluminous literature see Schrimpff (1989:79–100); Buchler and Maddock (1978); Luckert (1976); Allaire (1981:8–20); Barbeau (1967); Drummond (1981); Bassie-Sweet (1991); Semeka-Pankratov (1979); Tyler (1964:chap. 11); Carlson (1982).

2. White, red, yellow menses produced white, red, yellow turtles, respectively; black menses and red menses produced black and red monkeys, respectively; blue menses yielded a large number of plants.

3. Further discussion of color in Kuna texts may be found in Helms (1993b:242–244).

4. I believe that the question of whether or not the Coclé polychromes were used before they were interred is impossible to answer with certainty. The ceramics were originally coated with a vegetal varnish, and any evidence of use most likely would have been left on that coating. Since the coating could not be preserved, direct evidence of possible use in terms of abrasions or wear patterns is lost.

5. Conceivably the trampling of ceramics at elite mortuary rites replaced a more gruesome form of human sacrifice practiced in earlier times. It is also appropriate to note in this context the correspondence mentioned above for the Tukano (chap. 2) between the brightly colored boa and the joy of dancing.

6. "If I could tell you what it meant, there would be no point in dancing it" (qtd. in Bateson 1972:137).

REFERENCES

Allaire, Louis
   1981   The Saurian Pineal Eye in Antillean Art and Mythology. Journal of
           Latin American Lore 7:3–22.
Allen, Glover M.
   1942   Extinct and Vanishing Mammals of the Western Hemisphere with
           the Marine Species of all the Oceans. Special Publication No. 11.
           American Committee for International Wild Life Protection. [No
           further publication info. given. Committee commissioned by U.S.
           Government].
Bailey, L. H.
   1917   The Standard Cyclopedia of Horticulture. Vol. 6. New York:
           Macmillan Co.
Baker, Mary
   1992   Capuchin Monkeys (*Cebus capucinus*) and the Ancient Maya.
           Ancient Mesoamerica 3:219–228.
Barbeau, Marius
   1967   The Old-World Dragon in America. *In* Indian Tribes of
           Aboriginal America. Sol Tax, ed. Pp. 115–122. New York: Cooper
           Square Publishers.
Barton, Samuel, and William Barton
   1943   A Guide to the Constellations. New York: Whittlesey House.
Bassie-Sweet, Karen
   1991   From the Mouth of the Dark Cave. Norman: University of
           Oklahoma Press.
Bateson, Gregory
   1972   Style, Grace, and Information in Primitive Art. *In* Steps to an
           Ecology of Mind. Gregory Bateson. Pp. 128–152. New York:
           Ballantine Books.

Bennett, Charles F.

1968   Human Influences on the Zoogeograpy of Panama. Ibero-
                 Americana No. 51. Berkeley: University of California Press.

Berrin, Kathleen, ed.

1978   Art of the Huichol Indians. New York: Harry N. Abrams and the
                 Fine Arts Museum of San Francisco.

Bertin, Léon, et al.

1980   The New Larousse Encyclopedia of Animal Life. New York:
                 Bonanza Books.

Boinski, Sue

1992   Monkeys with Inflated Sex Appeal. Natural History Vol. 101
                 (July):42–49.

Bozzoli de Wille, Eugenia, and Carmen Cubero

1988   Una inversión de la historia talamanqueña del origen del mar. *In*
                 Primer seminario de tradicion e historia oral. Juan Rafael Quesada
                 Camacho, ed. Universidad de Costa Rica, facultad de Ciencias
                 Sociales. San José, C.R.: Ciudad Universitaria Rodrigo Facio.

Brown, James A.

1985   The Mississippian Period. *In* Ancient Art of the American
                 Woodland Indians. David Brose, James Brown, and David Penney.
                 Pp. 93–146. New York: Harry N. Abrams, Inc. in association with
                 The Detroit Institute of Arts.

Buchler, Ira, and Kenneth Maddock

1978   The Rainbow Serpent: A Chromatic Piece. The Hague: Mouton
                 Publishers.

Campbell, Alan T.

1989   To Square with Genesis. Iowa City: University of Iowa Press.

Campbell, Bruce, and Elizabeth Lack

1985   A Dictionary of Birds. Vermillion, S.D.: Buteo Books.

Campbell, Joseph

1959   The Masks of God: Primitive Mythology. New York: The Viking
                 Press.

Carlson, John B.

1982   The Double-Headed Dragon and the Sky. *In* Ethnoastronomy and
                 Archaeoastronomy in the American Tropics. Anthony F. Aveni and
                 Gary Urton, eds. Pp. 135–163. Annals of the New York Academy of
                 Sciences. Vol 385. New York: The New York Academy of Sciences.

Carr, Archie

1967   So Excellent a Fishe. New York: The Natural History Press.

Classen, Constance

1990   Sweet Colors, Fragrant Songs: Sensory Models of the Andes and
                 the Amazon. American Ethnologist 17:722–735.

Conzemius, Eduard

1932   Ethnographical Survey of the Miskito and Sumu Indians of
        Honduras and Nicaragua. Smithsonian Institution, Bureau of
        American Ethnology Bulletin No. 106. Washington, D.C.: U.S.
        Government Printing Office.

Cooke, Richard G.

1984   Archaeological Research in Central and Eastern Panama: A
        Review of Some Problems. *In* The Archaeology of Lower Central
        America. Frederick W. Lange and Doris Z. Stone, eds. Pp. 263–302.
        Albuquerque: University of New Mexico Press.

1985   Ancient Painted Pottery from Central Panama. Archaeology
        38:33–39.

1993   Animal Icons and Pre-Columbian Society: The Felidae, with
        Special Reference to Panama. *In* Reinterpreting Prehistory of
        Central America. Mark Miller Graham, ed. Pp. 169–208. Niwot,
        Co.: University Press of Colorado.

Coomaraswamy, Ananda K.

1935   The Transformation of Nature in Art. Cambridge: Harvard
        University Press.

Crocker, J. Christopher

1969   Reciprocity and Hierarchy Among the Eastern Bororo. Man
        4:44–58.

Dade, Philip L.

1961   The Provenience of Polychrome Pottery in Panama. Ethnos
        26:172–197.

David, Nicholas, Judy Sterner, and Kodzo Gavua

1988   Why Pots are Decorated. Current Anthropology 29:365–389.

de Civirieux, Marc

1980   Watunna: An Orinoco Creation Cycle. David M. Guss, ed. and
        trans. San Francisco: North Point Press.

Delacour, Jean, and Dean Amadon

1973   Currassows and Related Birds. New York: The American Museum
        of Natural History.

Douglas, Mary

1975   Implicit Meanings. London: Routledge and Kegan Paul.

Drummon, Lee

1981   The Serpent's Children: Semiotics of Cultural Genesis in Arawak
        and Trobriand Myth. American Ethnologist 8:633–660.

Easby, Elizabeth, and John Scott

1970   Before Cortes. New York: The Metropolitan Museum of Art.

Eco, Umberto

1986   Art and Beauty in the Middle Ages. Hugh Bredin, trans. New
        Haven: Yale University Press.

Eger, Susan, in collaboration with Peter R. Collings
1978   Huichol Women's Art. *In* Art of the Huichol Indians. Kathleen
        Berrin, ed. Pp. 35–53. New York: Harry N. Abrams and the Fine
        Arts Museum of San Francisco.

Emmons, Louise H.
1990   Neotropical Rainforest Mammals. Chicago: University of Chicago
        Press.

Fernandez, James W.
1973   The Exposition and Imposition of Order: Artistic Expression in
        Fang Culture. *In* The Traditional Artist in African Societies. Warren
        L. d'Azevedo, ed. Pp. 194–220. Bloomington: Indiana University
        Press.

Fowler, William R., Jr.
1989   The Cultural Evolution of Ancient Nahua Civilizations: The Pipil-
        Nicarao of Central America. Norman: University of Oklahoma
        Press.

Freidel, David, Linda Schele, and Joy Parker
1993   Maya Cosmos: Three Thousand Years on the Shaman's Path. New
        York: William Morrow and Co.

Furst, Peter, T.
1974   Hallucinogens in Precolumbian Art. *In* Art and Environment in
        Native America. Mary Elizabeth King and Idris R. Traylor, Jr., eds.
        Pp. 55–101. The Museum, Texas Tech University, Special
        Publication No. 7. Lubbock, Tx.: Texas Tech Press.
1978   The Art of "Being Huichol." *In* Art of the Huichol Indians.
        Kathleen Berrin, ed. Pp. 18–34. New York: Harry N. Abrams and
        the Fine Arts Museum of San Francisco.
1991   Crowns of Power: Bird and Feather Symbolism in Amazonian
        Shamanism. *In* The Gift of Birds: Featherwork of Native South
        American Peoples. Ruben E. Reina and Kenneth M. Kensinger,
        eds. Pp. 92–109. Philadelphia: University Museum of Archaeology
        and Anthropology, University of Pennsylvania.

Gilmore, Raymond M.
1950   Fauna and Ethnozoology of South America. Handbook of South
        American Indians. Julian H. Steward, ed. Pp. 345–464. Physical
        Anthropology, Linguistics, and Cultural Geography of South
        American Indians. Vol. 6. Washington, D.C.: U.S. Government
        Printing Office.

Goldman, Irving
1975   The Mouth of Heaven. New York: John Wiley and Sons.

González Cháves, Alfredo, and Fernando González Vásquez
1989   La casa cósmica talamanqueña y sus simbolismos. San José, Costa

Rica: Editorial de la Universidad de Costa Rica, Editorial
Universidad Estatal a Distancia.

Greene, H.W.
1983   *Boa Constrictor* (Boa, Béquer, Boa Constrictor) *In* Costa Rican
Natural History. Daniel H. Janzen, ed. Pp. 380–382. Chicago:
University of Chicago Press.

Guevara-Berger, Marcos
1993   A Visit to a Bribri Shaman. *In* South and Meso-American Native
Spirituality. Gary H. Gossen, ed. Pp. 371–389. New York: Crossroad.

Hall, E. Raymond, and Keith R. Kelson
1959   The Mammals of North America. Vol. 2. New York: The Ronald
Press Co.

Hallowell, A. I.
1926   Bear Ceremonialism in the Northern Hemisphere. American
Anthropologist 28:1–175.

Harter, Jim
1979   Animals: 1419 Copyright-Free Illustrations of Mammals, Birds, Fish,
Insects, etc. New York: Dover Publications, Inc.

Hayans, Guillermo
1952   New Cuna Myths. S. Henry Wassén, trans. Ethnologiska Studier
(Göteborg) 20:85–105.

Hearne, Pamela
1992   The Story of the River of Gold. *In* River of Gold: Precolumbian
Treasures from Sitio Conte. Pamela Hearne and Robert Sharer, eds.
Pp. 1–21. Philadelphia: The University Museum, University of
Pennsylvania.

Hearne, Pamela, and Robert Sharer, eds.
1992   River of Gold: Precolumbian Treasures from Sitio Conte.
Philadelphia: The University Museum, University of Pennsylvania.

Helms, Mary W.
1977   Iguanas and Crocodilians in Tropical American Mythology and
Iconography with Special Reference to Panama. Journal of Latin
American Lore 3:51–132.

1979   Ancient Panama. Austin: University of Texas Press.

1981   Cuna Molas and Coclé Art Forms. Philadelphia: Institute for the
Study of Human Issues.

1992   Cosmovision of the Chiefdoms of the Isthmus of Panama. *In* The
Ancient Americas: Art from Sacred Landscapes. Richard F.
Townsend, ed. Pp. 217–227. Chicago: The Art Institute of Chicago.

1993a   Craft and the Kingly Ideal. Austin: University of Texas Press.

1993b   Cosmological Chromatics: Color-Related Symbolism in the
Ceramic Art of Ancient Panama. *In* Reinterpreting Prehistory of

Central America. Mark Miller Graham, ed. Pp. 209–252. Niwot, Co.: University Press of Colorado.

Hill, Jane H.
  1992   The Flower World of Old Uto-Aztecan. Journal of Anthropological Research 48:117–144.

Hill, Jonathan D., and Robin M. Wright
  1988   Time, Narrative, and Ritual: Historical Interpretations from an Amazonian Society. *In* Rethinking History and Myth. Jonathan D. Hill, ed. Pp. 78–105. Urbana: University of Illinois Press.

Hilty, Steven L., and William L. Brown
  1986   A Guide to the Birds of Colombia. Princeton: Princeton University Press.

Holloman, Regina
  1969   Developmental Change in San Blas. Ph.D. dissertation, Northwestern University.

Howard, Catherine V.
  1991   Fragments of the Heavens: Feathers as Ornaments Among the Waiwai. *In* The Gift of Birds: Featherwork of Native South American Peoples. Ruben E. Reina and Kenneth M. Kensinger, eds. Pp. 50–69. Philadelphia: University Museum of Archaeology and Anthropology, University of Pennsylvania.

Howe, James
  1974   Village Political Organization among the San Blas Cuna. Ph.D. dissertation, University of Pennsylvania.
  1975   "Carrying the Village: Cuna Political Metaphors," Manuscript.
  1986   The Kuna Gathering: Contemporary Village Politics in Panama. Austin: University of Texas Press.

Hugh-Jones, Christine
  1977   Skin and Soul: The Round and the Straight. Social Time and Social Space in Pira-Parana Society. *In* Social Time and Social Space in Lowland South American Societies. Joanna Overing-Kaplan, organizer. Pp. 185–204. Actes XLII Congres International des Americanistes. Vol II. Paris.

Hugh-Jones, Stephen
  1979   The Palm and The Pleiades. Cambridge: Cambridge University Press.
  1982   The Pleiades and Scorpius in Barasana Cosmology. *In* Ethnoastronomy and Archaeoastronomy in the American Tropics. Anthony F. Aveni and Gary Urton, eds. Pp. 183–201. Annals of the New York Academy of Sciences. Vol 385. New York: The New York Academy of Sciences.

Hunt, Eva
  1977   The Transformation of the Hummingbird. Ithaca: Cornell University Press.

Ingold, Tim
  1987   The Appropriation of Nature. Iowa City: University of Iowa Press.

Janick, Jules, et al.
  1981   Plant Science: An Introduction to World Crops. 3rd ed. San Francisco: W. H. Freeman and Co.

Karsten, Rafael
 [1926]
  1968   The Civilization of the South American Indians. London: Kegan Paul, Trench, Trubner and Co.

Kaufman, John H.
  1982   Raccoon and Allies (*Procyon lotor* and Allies). *In* Wild Mammals of North America. Joseph Chapman and George Feldhamer, eds. Pp. 567–585. Baltimore: Johns Hopkins University Press.

Kirchhoff, Paul
  1948   The Tribes North of the Orinoco River. *In* Handbook of South American Indians. Vol 4. The Circum-Caribbean Tribes. Julian H. Steward, ed. Pp. 481–493. Washington, D.C.: U.S. Government Printing Office.

Koopman, Karl F.
  1991   Bear. *In* The Encyclopedia Americana. Vol. 3 of 30 vols. Pp. 398–400. Danbury, Conn.: Grolier Inc.

Labbé, Armand J.
  1986   Colombia Before Columbus. New York: Rizzoli International Publishers.

Lancaster, D. A.
  1983   *Crypturellus cinnamomeus* (Tinamú Canelo, Gongolona, Gallina de Monte, Rufescent Tinamou). *In* Costa Rican Natural History. Daniel H. Janzen, ed. Pp. 572–573. Chicago: The University of Chicago Press.

Landa, Friar Diego de
  1978   Yucatan Before and After the Conquest. William Gates, trans. New York: Dover Publishing Inc.

Lechtman, Heather
  1975   Style in Technology—Some Early Thoughts. *In* Material Culture: Styles, Organization, and Dynamics of Technology. H. Lechtman and R. S. Merrill, eds. Pp. 3–20. 1975 Proceedings of the American Ethnological Society. St. Paul: West Publishing Co.
  1979   Issues in Andean Metallurgy. *In* Pre-Columbian Metallurgy of South America. E. P. Benson, ed. Pp. 1–40. Washington, D.C.: Dumbarton Oaks Research Library and Collections.

Lévi-Strauss, Claude
  1964   Tristes Tropiques. John Russell, trans. New York: Atheneum.
  1969   The Raw and the Cooked. New York: Harper and Row.
  1973   From Honey to Ashes. New York: Harper and Row.

1978   The Origin of Table Manners. New York: Harper and Row.

1988   The Jealous Potter. Chicago: University of Chicago Press.

Linares, Olga F.

1977   Ecology and the Arts in Panama: On the Development of Social
        Rank and Symbolism in the Central Provinces. Dumbarton Oaks
        Studies in Pre-Columbian Art and Archaeology No. 17.
        Washington, D.C.: Dumbarton Oaks.

Locher, Gottfried W.

1932   The Serpent in Kwakiutl Religion. Leyden: E. J. Brill.

Lothrop, Samuel K.

1942   Coclé: An Archaeological Study of Central Panama. Part II.
        Pottery of the Sitio Conte and other Archaeological Sites. Vol VIII.
        Memoirs, Peabody Museum of Archaeology and Ethnology.
        Cambridge, Mass.: Peabody Museum of Archaeology and
        Ethnology, Harvard University.

1964   Treasures of Ancient America. Geneva: Skira.

1976   Pre-Columbian Designs from Panama: 591 Illustrations of Coclé
        Pottery. New York: Dover Publications.

Luckert, Karl W.

1976   Olmec Religion. Norman: University of Oklahoma Press.

Mason, Peter

1990   Deconstructing America. London: Routledge.

McDowell, John H.

1989   Sayings of the Ancestors: The Spiritual Life of the Sibundoy
        Indians. Lexington: University of Kentucky Press.

Miller, Mary, and Karl Taube

1993   The Gods and Symbols of Ancient Mexico and the Maya. New
        York: Thames and Hudson.

Morphy, Howard, ed.

1989   Animals Into Art. London: Unwin Hyman.

Morphy, Howard

1991   Ancestral Connections. Chicago: University of Chicago Press.

Nordenskiöld, Erland

[1925]

1979   An Historical and Ethnological Survey of the Cuna Indians. Henry
        Wassén, ed. Reprinted New York: AMS Press. [Comparative
        Ethnological Studies No. 10, Götenborg Museum, Götenborg,
        Sweden].

Pauketat, Timothy R., and Thomas E. Emerson

1991   The Ideology of Authority and the Power of the Pot. American
        Anthropologist 93:919–941.

Penney, David W.

1985   Continuities of Imagery and Symbolism in the Art of the

Woodlands. *In* Ancient Art of the American Woodland Indians. David Brose, James Brown, and David Penney. Pp. 147–198. New York: Harry N. Abrams, Inc. in association with The Detroit Institute of Arts.

Pressman, Jon F.

1991   Feathers of Blood and Fire: The Mythological Origins of Avian Coloration. *In* The Gift of Birds: Featherwork of Native South American Peoples. Ruben E. Reina and Kenneth M. Kensinger, eds. Pp. 78–91. Philadelphia: University Museum of Archaeology and Anthropology, University of Pennsylvania.

Rabineau, Phyllis

1975   Artists and Leaders: The Social Context of Creativity in a Tropical Rain Forest Culture. *In* The Cashinahua of Eastern Peru. Kenneth M. Kensinger, et al. Pp. 87–109. Brown University, Haffenreffer Museum of Anthropology.

Reichel-Dolmatoff, Gerardo

1971   Amazonian Cosmos. Chicago: University of Chicago Press.

1972   The Cultural Context of an Aboriginal Hallucinogen: *Banisteriopsis caapi*. *In* Flesh of the Gods: The Ritual Use of Hallucinogens. Peter T. Furst, ed. Pp. 84–113. New York: Praeger Publisher.

1975   The Shaman and the Jaguar. Philadelphia: Temple University Press.

1978a   Desana Animal Categories, Food Restrictions, and the Concept of Color Energies. Journal of Latin American Lore 4:243–291.

1978b   Beyond the Milky Way. UCLA Latin American Center Publications. Los Angeles: University of California.

1982   Astronomical Models of Social Behavior Among Some Indians of Colombia. *In* Ethnoastronomy and Archaeoastronomy in the American Tropics. Anthony F. Aveni and Gary Urton, eds. Pp. 165–181. Annals of the New York Academy of Sciences. Vol 385. New York: The New York Academy of Sciences.

1985   Tapir Avoidance in the Colombian Northwest Amazon. *In* Animal Myths and Metaphors in South America. Gary Urton, ed. Pp. 107–143. Salt Lake City: University of Utah Press.

Ridgely, Robert S., and John A. Gwynne, Jr.

1989   A Guide to the Birds of Panama with Costa Rica, Nicaragua, and Honduras. 2nd ed. Princeton: Princeton University Press.

Ripinsky-Naxon, Michael

1993   The Nature of Shamanism. Albany: State University of New York Press.

Robicsek, Francis

1978   The Smoking Gods. Norman: University of Oklahoma Press.

Roe, Peter G.

1988   The Josho Nahuanbo are all Wet and Uncooked: Shipibo Views of the Whiteman and the Incas in Myth, Legend, and History. *In* Rethinking History and Myth. Jonathan D. Hill, ed. Pp. 106–135. Urbana: University of Illinois Press.

1989   Of Rainbow Dragons and the Origins of Design: The Waiwai and the Shipibo Ronin Ehua. Latin American Indian Literatures Journal 5:1–67.

Rowe, John H.

1962   Chávin Art: An Inquiry into its Form and Meaning. New York: Museum of Primitive Art.

1967   Form and Meaning in Chávin Art. *In* Peruvian Archaeology: Selected Readings. John H. Rowe and Dorothy Menzel, eds. Pp. 72–103. Palo Alto, Ca.: Peek Publication.

Sauer, Carl O.

1950   Cultivated Plants of South and Central America. *In* Physical Anthropology, Linguistics, and Cultural Geography of South American Indians. Pp. 487–543. Handbook of South American Indians, vol. 6. Washington, D.C.: U.S. Government Printing Office.

1966   The Early Spanish Main. Berkeley: University of California Press.

Schele, Linda, and David Freidel

1990   A Forest of Kings. New York: William Morrow and Co.

Schele, Linda, and Mary Ellen Miller

1986   The Blood of Kings. New York: George Braziller, Inc.

Schmidt, Karl P., and Robert F. Inger

1957   Living Reptiles of the World. Garden City, N.Y.: Doubleday.

Schorger, A. W.

1966   The Wild Turkey: Its History and Domestication. Norman: University of Oklahoma Press.

Schrimpff, Marianne

1989   The Snake and the Fabulous Beast: Themes from the Pottery of the Ilama Culture. *In* Animals Into Art. Howard Morphy, ed. Pp. 75–108. London: Unwin Hyman.

Schultes, Richard Evans

1972   An Overview of Hallucinogens in the Western Hemisphere. *In* Flesh of the Gods: The Ritual Use of Hallucinogens. Peter T. Furst, ed. Pp. 3–54. New York: Praeger Publisher.

1984   Amazonian Cultigens and Their Northward and Westward Migrations in Pre-Columbian Times. *In* Pre-Columbian Plant Migration. Doris Stone, ed. Pp. 20–37. Papers of the Peabody Museum of Archaeology and Ethnology. Vol. 76. Cambridge, Mass.: Peabody Museum of Archaeology and Ethnology, Harvard University.

Schultes, Richard Evans, and Alec Bright

1981   Ancient Gold Pectorals from Colombia: Mushroom Effigies? *In*
        Sweat of the Sun, Tears of the Moon: Gold and Emerald Treasures
        of Colombia. Essays by Peter T. Furst, et al. Pp. 37–43. Los Angeles:
        Terra Magazine Publications and the Natural History Museum
        Alliance of Los Angeles County.

Semeka-Pankratov, Elena

1979   A Semiotic Approach to the Polysemy of the Symbol *nāga* in
        Indian Mythology. Semiotica 27:237–290.

Shepard, Paul, and Barry Sanders

1985   The Sacred Paw: The Bear in Nature, Myth, and Literature. New
        York: Viking.

Sherzer, Dina, and Joel Sherzer

1976   Mormaknamaloe: The Cuna Mola. *In* Ritual and Symbol in
        Native Central America. Philip Young and James Howe, eds. Pp.
        21–42. University of Oregon Anthropological Papers No. 9.
        Eugene, Or.

Sherzer, Joel

1974   Namakke, Sunmakke, Karmakke: Three Types of Cuna Speech
        Event. *In* Exploration in the Ethnography of Speaking. R. Bauman
        and J. Sherzer, eds. Pp. 263–282. London: Cambridge University
        Press.

1983   Kuna Ways of Speaking. Austin: University of Texas Press.

Skutch, Alexander F.

1983   Birds of Tropical America. Austin: University of Texas Press.

Stewart, Hilary

1979   Looking at Indian Art of the Northwest Coast. Vancouver: Douglas
        and McIntyre.

Stone, Doris

1962   The Talamancan Tribes of Costa Rica. Papers of the Peabody
        Museum of Archaeology and Ethnology. Vol. 42. Cambridge, Mass.:
        Peabody Museum of Archaeology and Ethnology, Harvard
        University.

1967   Living Archaeology of the Bribri and Cabécar Indians of Costa
        Rica. *In* Indian Tribes of Aboriginal America. Sol Tax, ed. Pp.
        251–253. New York: Cooper Square Publishers.

1977   Pre-Columbian Man in Costa Rica. Cambridge, Mass.: Peabody
        Museum of Archaeology and Ethnology, Harvard University.

1984   Pre-Columbian Migration of *Theobroma cacao* Linnaeus and
        Manihot esculenta Crantz from Northern South America into
        Mesoamerica: A Partially Hypothetical View. *In* Pre-Columbian
        Plant Migration. Doris Stone, ed. Pp. 68–83. Papers of the Peabody

Museum of Archaeology and Ethnology. Vol. 76. Cambridge, Mass.: Peabody Museum of Archaeology and Ethnology, Harvard University.

Stout, David B.

[1964]

1947   San Blas Cuna Acculturation: An Introduction. Viking Fund Publications in Anthropology No. 9. New York: The Viking Fund. [Reprint New York: Johnson Reprint Corp.]

Tacon, Paul S. C.

1989   Art and the Essence of Being: Symbolic and Economic Aspects of Fish among the Peoples of Western Arnhem Land, Australia. *In* Animals Into Art. Howard Morphy, ed. Pp. 236–250. London: Unwin Hyman.

Taussig, Michael

1980   Folk Healing and the Structure of Conquest in Southwest Colombia. Journal of Latin American Lore 6:217–278.

1987   Shamanism, Colonialism, and the Wild Man. Chicago: University of Chicago Press.

Tedlock, Barbara

1984   The Beautiful and the Dangerous: Zuni Ritual and Cosmology as an Aesthetic System. Conjunctions 6:246–265.

Thompson, J. Eric S.

1970   Maya History and Religion. Norman: University of Oklahoma Press.

Tuzin, Donald F.

1978   Politics, Power, and Divine Artistry in Ilahita. Anthropological Quarterly 51:61–67.

Tyler, Hamilton A.

1964   Pueblo Gods and Myths. Norman: University of Oklahoma Press.

1975   Pueblo Animals and Myths. Norman: University of Oklahoma Press.

Urton, Gary

1985   Animal Metaphors and The Life Cycle in an Andean Community. *In* Animal Myths and Metaphors in South America. Gary Urton, ed. Pp. 251–284. Salt Lake City: University of Utah Press.

Van Gelder, Richard G.

1990   Bear. *In* Collier's Encyclopedia. Vol. 3 of 24 vols. P. 733. New York: Macmillan.

Van Rosen, Beatrice

1990   Mammals. Collier's Encyclopedia. Pp. 294–316. New York: Macmillan.

Vansina, Jan

1985   Oral Tradition as History. Madison: University of Wisconsin Press.

Walker, Ernest P., et al.

1975a   Mammals of the World. 3rd ed., Vol. 2. Baltimore: Johns Hopkins
University Press.

1975b   Mammals of the World. 3rd ed., Vol. 1. Baltimore: Johns Hopkins
University Press.

Wassén, S. Henry

1965   The Use of Some Specific Kinds of South American Indian Snuff
and Related Paraphernalia. Etnologiska Studier #28. Göteborg
Etnografiska Museet.

1967   Anthropological Survey of the Use of South American Snuffs. *In*
Ethnopharmacologic Search for Psychoactive Drugs. Daniel H.
Efron, ed. Pp. 233–289. Public Health Service Publication No. 1645,
United States Department of Health, Education and Welfare.
Washington, D.C.: U.S. Government Printing Office.

Weinhardt, Diana

1993   The Spectacled Bear. *In* Bears: Majestic Creatures of the Wild. Ian
Stirling, ed. Pp. 134–139. Emmaus, Pa.: Rodale Press.

Wetmore, Alexander

1965   The Birds of the Republic of Panama. Part I: *Tinamidae (Tinamous)
to Rynchopidae (Skimmers)*. Smithsonian Miscellaneous Collections.
Vol 150. Washington, D.C.: Smithsonian Institution.

Whitley, David S.

1993   Shamanism, Natural Modeling, and Far Western North American
Hunter-Gatherers. *In* The Briefing Book for Cosmology and
Natural Modeling Among Aboriginal American Peoples. The
Second D. J. Sibley Conference on World Traditions of Culture
and Art. Pp. 2–18. Department of Art and College of Fine Arts,
University of Texas, Austin.

Whitten, Dorothea S., and Norman E. Whitten, Jr.

1988   From Myth to Creation. Urbana: University of Illinois Press.

Wilbert, Johannes

1972   Tobacco and Shamanistic Ecstasy Among the Warao Indians of
Venezuela. *In* Flesh of the Gods: The Ritual Use of Hallucinogens.
Peter T. Furst, ed. Pp. 55–83. New York: Praeger Publisher.

1987   Tobacco and Shamanism in South America. New Haven: Yale
University Press.

Zuidema, R. Tom

1985   The Lion in the City: Royal Symbols of Transition in Cuzco. *In*
Animal Myths and Metaphors in South America. Gary Urton, ed.
Pp. 183–250. Salt Lake City: University of Utah Press.

INDEX

Aesthetics, 7–8, 15
Agouti, 11, 53
Algarroba (*Prosopis juliflora or P. alba*), 74
Alice in Wonderland, 3, 109
Amazon, 9–10, 13, 32, 64, 86, 104
Anaconda: ancestors and, 84; as Celestial Dragon, 101; compared to boa, 19; eating habits of, 86; skin color of, 101; writing on, 108
Anadenanthera colubrina, 74, 80
Ancestors, 70, 84, 100, 107–9
Anteaters, 11, 26–27, 33, 53
Appendages, 53–54, 71
Arecuna, 11
Art: cosmology and, 6, 77–78, 85, 108; in Panamanian life, 15, 108–9; politics and, 3, 5–7, 15, 107–9
Artisans, 7, 8, 13, 85
Australia, 106, 107–8
Authority, political, 7, 106–7
Ayahuasca, 45. *See also* Yagé

Banisteriopsis, 45, 80, 81
Bear, 59–69, 85; Andean or Spectacled (*Tremarctos ornatus*), 53, 59, 71, 73; Bear Mother, 67; as Master of Animals, 69; paws motif, 76; Bear Sons, 67; zoological features of, 59–60
Belize, 88
Birds, 33, 74; appendages and, 54; clay-eating, 50; color coding of, 51; crested, 29; galliform, 54; head crests of, 39, 83; Mother of, 46, 47; origins of, 22; as serpent-derived, 16–17; with severed leg, 33, 83; with wattles, 39–40, 48, 50, 51; zoological features of, 39

Blood and coloration theme: anaconda and, 101; on bird symbols, 17; body openings and, 86; child in sky myth of, 84; eagles and, 41; from formlessness, 11; from mythological sloth, 29; mytheme of, 11–12; serpent as source of, 22–23; sloth and, 70; severed-leg theme and, 46; solar-related serpent themes and, 106; and Tree of Life, 77
Blood, 22, 23, 79, 84, 106
Boa: anaconda and, 39; as design motif, 81; luminosity and, 101; markings, 76; Miskito tale of, 106; oval, 21–22, 76, 78, 87, 96, 98; as primary isthmian version of Great Serpent, 32; Sumu myth of, 79; zoological features of, 18–19, 101. *See also* Serpent, Great Serpent
Bodily orifices, 86, 87
Boráro, 64
Bororo, 93
Brazil, 27, 93, 108; Mato Grosso, 70
Bribri, 30
Brilliance, 99–101, 105
Burial: of ceramics, 107–8; of elites, 3, 8, 15, 107, 108
Bushmaster (*Lachesia muta*), 31

Cacao (*Theobroma cacao*), 74–78, 91, 95, 98; and Tree of Life, 77
Caduveo, 11–12
Capybara, 53
Cat, ring-tailed, 53, 66. *See also* Coati
Ceiba (or silkcotton) (*Ceiba pentandra*), 74, 76, 79
Ceramics: buried, 107–8; significance of forms, 79, 97–99; trampled, 108–9